MW01615776

Seasons of a Soul-preneur

How to Embrace Your Circle
of Growth as a Small Business Owner

Stephanie Ross

Soul-preneur Definition

An entrepreneur who intentionally builds their business around their soul purpose and in alignment with their values to make a positive impact on those they serve

To every small business owner willing to weather the seasons of soul-preneurship.

May this book be the mentor you didn't know you needed, and the reminder to embrace all the mountains and valleys along your journey. Trust your nudges and let your soul inspire your strategy.

To my husband, sister, mom & dad: Thank you for always listening to my audacious dreams and supporting every season of my own soul-preneur journey–I wouldn't have made it through without you.

To Val: May you feel encouraged, supported, and empowered to chase your own dreams and always let your soul be your north star.

Praise for Seasons of a Soul-preneur

"In a world obsessed with hustle, Seasons of a Soul-preneur reminds us that the real growth happens in the quiet, messy middle. Few write about business with this much heart, vulnerability, and spiritual depth. A must-read for soul-driven entrepreneurs."

—Lindsey Marie, Founder of Powerhouse Women

"What more entrepreneurs need to hear is the rare honesty of the seasons in business. It's not all sunshine and success, nor doom and gloom. Knowing when it's time to plant, water, and harvest your plans and ideas is the key to riding the inevitable entrepreneurship waves. Stephanie did an excellent job shedding light on and giving hope to the journey!"

—Ashley Alderson, Founder and CEO, The Boutique Hub & Hubventory

"Watching Stephanie navigate the real-life highs and lows of soulful entrepreneurship has been truly inspiring. Her willingness to learn through adversity, lead with integrity, and lift others as she climbs speaks to the powerful ripple effect of women supporting women in business. Soul-preneurship, at its best, is not just about building a business—it's about building a life of purpose and legacy. Stephanie's done that!"

—Misty Lown, Founder of More Than Just Great DancingTM and Misty's Dance Unlimited

"I was surprisingly moved by the book itself. Stephanie and I have many things in common — the biggest difference is she is a quarter of a century younger than me! I see myself in her, and then some! Stephanie has the ability to bring people together and celebrate life's big and small, short and long challenges, failures, mistakes and beauty all simultaneously. This book portrays all of that very well and illustrates turning life lessons into success. Stephanie makes it look easy."

—Debra Lash-Stangel, Founder of The Wedding Tree, The Court Above Main, The La Crosse Wedding Expo

"Seasons of a Soul-preneur is the guide I wish I had in my own entrepreneurial journey. Stephanie doesn't just tell her story—she creates a safe space for all of us who've poured everything into a dream and found ourselves running on empty. This book meets you where you are—whether you're planting seeds, pushing through the storm, or trying to find the strength to begin again. With heart, grit, and truth, Stephanie reminds us that our setbacks are sacred ground for growth. You'll leave these pages feeling seen, supported, and ready to take fierce action toward your next season.

–Dr. Carolyn Colleen Bostrack, Ph.D., Author, Speaker, Executive Leader, and Founder of the FIERCE Foundation

What do you do when chasing your dream leads straight into the heart of the storm?

Have you ever felt crushed by the very dream you were chasing? Stephanie Ross, founder of Small Business Sister Circle™, knows exactly what that feels like. After nearly a decade pouring every ounce of her energy into building her dream fitness and yoga studio, she found herself walking away, heartbroken and financially depleted. Yet, in the darkest moments of what she calls her entrepreneurial trauma, Stephanie discovered her greatest lessons and her true calling—guiding other female entrepreneurs through the inevitable cycles of small business ownership.

In *Seasons of a Soul-preneur*, soul meets strategy as Stephanie blends vulnerable storytelling with powerful, relatable lessons, taking you through the emotional and spiritual seasons every entrepreneur faces: Planting, Growing, Weathering the Storms, and Harvest. This book is not just about surviving entrepreneurship—it's about thriving through each season and using the challenges as fuel to reignite your passion and creativity along the way.

Whether you're navigating the valley of despair or looking forward to your harvest season, Stephanie's honest reflections and actionable insights will inspire you to embrace your entrepreneurial journey. It's time to turn your setbacks into soul-growing comebacks and fall in love with your business again.

Table of Contents

Table of Contents

Introduction

The Valley of Despair

This is not exactly where I thought I'd be by now, I kept thinking to myself. But I've learned that life is funny like that, with many twists and turns along the way. And while I'd always dreamt I'd be further along at the age of thirty, I realized that everything turns out exactly the way it's meant to be.

It was November 2022, and I was preparing for a month-long sabbatical from teaching fitness and yoga classes for my business, Zen and Pow Studio. I was walking around Barnes and Noble, looking for books that I felt would help me cope and heal from the trauma I had experienced. I was in the thick of the hardest, darkest, scariest chapter of business (and life), as I'd made, hands down, the hardest decision to walk away from my current brick-and-mortar studio space and business model after almost ten years of working endlessly. Now it was time to try something brand new.

To give you some insight, I have chased this dream since I was twenty. I gave every ounce of energy, time, and money to try and make this business work. When I'd moved into the studio space four years earlier, I'd thought it would be my big break in finding success in my business. But instead, it led to my *biggest* breaking point.

I'd paid for the build-out, and I knew I'd *still* be paying for the build-out years after deciding to leave the space. I'd given everything and all of my money for the last nine years to seeing my dream of having a fully operational, profitable, and sustainable studio come true.

Not only was I walking away from a space that I'd poured every hard-earned penny into, but it felt like I was walking away from my dream and the younger version of myself. It felt like I was letting people down along the way; my deepest hurt was disappointing my team, members, and, ultimately, myself.

I flat out felt like I failed. On every level. And worst—I'd done everything I could to keep the space and my dream alive.

When I sat down and did the numbers, it just didn't make sense. My monthly rent for this big, beautiful space and the business loan were eating up almost all of my income every month. I was scraping by, working more, and getting gritty to make up the rest. And, as you get to know me, you'll come to find that work ethic has never been my challenge.

But I was tired. Soul-level depleted.

Every month of that year got harder and harder, and I had reached my mental and physical breaking point. The truth was, I was tapped out financially too.

I had to come up with nearly $10,000 just to break even every month. And while I was so creative in the business's offerings, I had run out of ideas and energy. I had used every penny of grant money we'd received during the pandemic. And I had used up every penny in my personal savings to try and make this dream work.

And the worst part: I'd come to realize that working more wouldn't solve my problems. Something had to give. As much as my heart and head hated to admit it, the studio space needed to go.

It was time. If I wanted to continue to run my business, I had to find a better way.

So I got creative in my valley of despair—which is one of my secret geniuses (often by necessity)—and came up with a pop-up studio model. I would simply rent space at a few locations, cut back my schedule, offer what I know works and the classes people love, and get back to having fun in my business again! I was so burned out by this point that a pivot was essential.

Even though I knew this decision was the *right* decision, it didn't mean it was the *easy* decision. Isn't it funny how the right decision is often the most difficult to make? It was painful to let go.

It felt like rock bottom.

Believe me, I knew hardship from previous years of business— but nothing like this.

This was the bottom of the deepest, darkest valley.

To give everything you have and still not see something work out is an indescribable pain. Chances are, you've probably experienced this in your own small business journey at some point. We call it "entrepreneurial trauma." And, man, it's real.

I knew I needed time, introspection, and guidance to heal from this kind of trauma. So, as I meandered through Barnes and Noble—a secret favorite hobby of mine—I stumbled across a book: *Boundless Creativity: A Spiritual Workbook for Overcoming Self-Doubt, Emotional Traps, and Other Creative Blocks.*

Interesting, I thought. While I consider myself creative, the burden and stress of the season I was in had killed my own creativity. So I wanted to reignite that. I bought the book that day, not realizing it would be one of the best tools I could have ever purchased when it came to digging through my own Universal Story.

Fast-forward a few days: I taught my last class on Thanksgiving, celebrated my thirtieth birthday, moved all my things out, and turned in the keys to my once-upon-a-time dream space. Then the realization of what I'd just gone through finally sunk in. I was experiencing every emotion possible. So I finally opened up the workbook I bought and started to dig in.

I learned that the Universal Story is how we come to understand our own stories and our own lives. It is like climbing a mountain with four parts: Knowing Yourself, Sea of Creativity, Deep Dive, and The Prize. Among those four parts, there are dips of valleys in between—turning points, typically tragedy or hardship—that force you to overcome. The first is No Turning Back, followed by Recommitment, and then All Is Lost. Finally, you reach eventual Triumph. Seeing my path laid out in a logical way in this workbook really got my wheels turning.

It was then January 2023, and I dug in deeper. Thanks to the workbook, I committed to my creativity goal of doing what I've been talking about doing for years—writing *this book*!

Simultaneously, I was reading a book called *The 12 Week Year*, which brought to my attention the Emotional Cycle of Change. I realized that it was zeroing in on a turning point along the Universal Story and how we get through what is referred to as "the Valley of Despair" to reach higher ground.

Light bulbs were going on in my head, and I started teaching this concept to those around me, including fellow small business owners, because who hasn't been through a valley of despair? We all have! And again, it's about how you come out of it—better, instead of bitter—that matters.

By no coincidence, my friend Carolyn asked me to speak at her conference in February. As I was chatting with her about my topic, I threw out my usual business topics: productivity, business strategy, leadership . . .

"What I really want you to share, Stephanie, is your story," she said.

"My story?" I questioned. *Yikes—are you sure?* I thought. I'd been through so much over the past ten years of growing up with my business and coming out of my toughest season of entrepreneurship that I didn't even know where to begin. And I wasn't sure it was even that inspiring, considering what I'd just gone through. I felt like a failure.

"Yes, tell us about your entrepreneurial journey. It's inspiring!" she continued.

And then it hit me: Maybe, just maybe, it was more inspiring *because* of what I'd just gone through.

How many people have the courage to walk away from a dream with grace and their heads held high? I was hanging on by a thread in this season. Nonetheless, I was continuing to move forward despite my heartache, loss, and pain.

I was continuing to pivot, re-envision my life, and redefine success for myself, even amidst uncertainty.

She was asking *me* to share *my* story and be vulnerable, even though I was feeling far from a mountaintop moment. But I was no longer in the valley either—I had searched for higher ground. And I was climbing my way out.

Could I teach this? Could this be the whole purpose of my pain? To help people write their own Universal Story and how to move through the life cycles of small business ownership productively and peacefully, despite their loss and pain?

All of these little synchronicities are whispers from God. They are signs along the path telling me to keep going. Telling me that I'm onto something . . . and that God is guiding me along the way. This gave me the beginning of my talk about my story and my life journey through what I call "soul-preneurship." Because when you tune into yourself and your soul, you'll never go astray. Thanks to many nudges from my own soul, I finally found the courage to start this book.

I realized that not only would writing my story help me heal myself, but it could help so many others—especially small business owners like you!

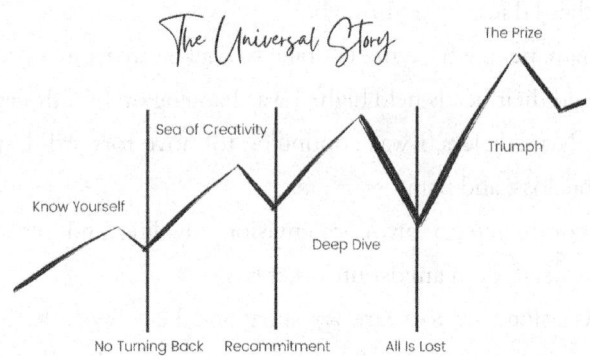

Universal Story graph

The Cycles and Seasons of Small Business Ownership

"Like the changing seasons, entrepreneurship has its ups and downs, periods of growth and stagnation, where the key is to adapt and weather each phase with resilience, knowing that just as winter gives way to spring, challenges will eventually lead to new opportunities."
— Unknown

Right before my rock-bottom season, I decided to take up gardening—because why not try to put my efforts somewhere else when it wasn't working for my business? My business wasn't growing, so maybe my vegetables would? Just kidding—but not really. Through this newfound passion, I realized that small business ownership—along with life, I guess you could say—is a lot like gardening.

You start by planting seeds and dreams of possibilities! This is the fun part of entrepreneurship, when you're just getting started and everything feels new and exciting. You grab a few seeds at the store (often without doing your research), throw them into the soil without much insight or intention, and yet are hopeful for the harvest they will bring. You can see your big dreams bright and clear for the future of your business. It's the perfect amount of naivety you need to get started.

Next comes the growing season, when you impatiently wait, water, and weed, still excited about what harvest your plants will bring. You hustle with heart over your garden each day just to see those little sprouts pop up. What will they become? You continue watering them daily, waiting and plucking out the dead leaves and any negativity that might come your way. You're embracing the joy of the grind in this season.

Many of us don't expect what often comes next, and it's the hardest season to prepare for—weathering the storms, droughts, and cycles. These are the challenges outside our own control that force us to show up in a whole new way, testing our commitment, our resiliency, and our hope for the future. Sometimes, it's a storm, like the pandemic; sometimes, it's a financial drought when business is down.

You have to remember that all businesses go through cycles and seasons of highs and lows, and you have to learn to embrace the ups and downs. The key to weathering the storm is not losing hope and trusting yourself to evolve, pivot, and push through, even when your vision of the harvest is no longer clearly visible. Sometimes, you have to start over and wait for a whole new planting, growing, and weathering-the-storm season to get to your harvest season—but you're always starting over with experience. *Not going to plant that one; my lettuce died last year because of too much sun. My green beans had an exceptional harvest; let's keep going with that one.*

I can assure you that I didn't have a green thumb when I started gardening. Just ask my mom; I killed every indoor house plant I was ever given. And my first two seasons of gardening didn't reap much of a harvest either. But by years three and four, I was starting to finally get some harvest going. As you'll find out in this book, it took me a decade to start to experience my harvest season in small business ownership. So, wherever you are on your small business journey today, keep going! The harvest season is worth the wait, and I promise that when you experience the growing season and weather the storms, you'll appreciate your harvest that much more.

While this is a how-to book, it isn't your typical how-to business book full of in-depth strategies to implement. Rather, this book shows you how to embrace the journey of soul growth through small business ownership. And it's broken into four seasons: planting, growing, weathering the storms, and harvesting. The stories I share are my own experiences through entrepreneurship, as business has been my vehicle for soul growth. I believe we all have a purpose for being here, and it is our purpose to learn the lessons we need along the way for our souls to grow. For me, that happens to be more or less the hard way—but that's just how it goes sometimes.

I've grown to thoroughly enjoy gardening over the last few years—not because I'm an expert and my harvest is now bountiful year after year but because I've come to enjoy the process of gardening and not knowing what each season will bring. Over the last decade, I've also come to enjoy the journey of small business ownership and the seasons, cycles, and new opportunities for growth that each new challenge brings.

Of course, I love picking out the seeds to plant each year, just as I love dreaming new dreams and ideas for my businesses. I've always loved the growing seasons of gardening and small business ownership. (Who doesn't?) But I've learned to become more patient and intentional with my watering, waiting, and weeding to build sustainable businesses that allow me to enjoy my life alongside it. What I've come to appreciate more than ever, though, is weathering the storms and trusting my intuition, knowing when to pivot, evolve, or try something new. Sometimes it works, and sometimes it doesn't. But, when you don't weather the storms and cycles of your garden and business, the harvest just doesn't hit like it does when you've gone through it.

That is why I believe our storms are sent to us for a reason—every single struggle, loss, and obstacle has led me right here to write this book. Without experiencing my own seasons of growing pains, storms, drought, and loss, there would be no full-circle story to share. No challenge to overcome. No triumph to be felt. And no book to write. For that, I wouldn't take a single thing back.

No matter what age or stage of business or life you find yourself in, I hope these pages resonate with you. I hope you see yourself in these stories of planting, growing, weathering the storms, and finding your harvest season too.

This is my story of soul-preneurship.

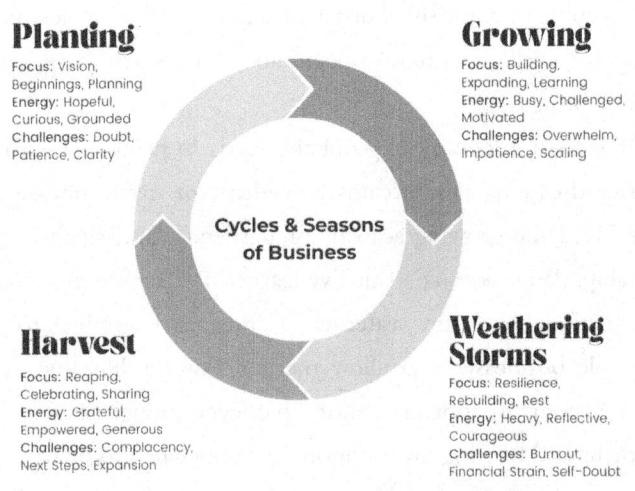

Planting
Focus: Vision, Beginnings, Planning
Energy: Hopeful, Curious, Grounded
Challenges: Doubt, Patience, Clarity

Growing
Focus: Building, Expanding, Learning
Energy: Busy, Challenged, Motivated
Challenges: Overwhelm, Impatience, Scaling

Cycles & Seasons of Business

Harvest
Focus: Reaping, Celebrating, Sharing
Energy: Grateful, Empowered, Generous
Challenges: Complacency, Next Steps, Expansion

Weathering Storms
Focus: Resilience, Rebuilding, Rest
Energy: Heavy, Reflective, Courageous
Challenges: Burnout, Financial Strain, Self-Doubt

Cycles and Seasons of business depicted
in Seasons of a Soul-preneur

Part 1: Planting

"The day you plant the seed is not the day you eat the fruit. Be patient and stay the course."

— Fabienne Fredrickson

Chapter 1:

Small Town with Big Dreams

Big Dreams with Small-Town Roots

I can't be the only kid from the rural Midwest who felt like their dreams were too big for the small town they grew up in. Who never wanted to follow the traditional rules of society: go to college, get married, get a good-paying job, work until retirement, enjoy the last ten years of life, and be content.

That didn't sit right with you either? Welcome; you've found your people.

I grew up in a humble home in southwest Wisconsin, but it was a home full of love and memories. I was blessed with two wonderful parents, and I could not imagine a better childhood. I look back with very fond memories of my youth—always playing, learning, and creating.

I was the product of two entrepreneurial parents who, I believe, only encouraged and ignited the entrepreneurial spirit in both my sister and me further. Not only that, they are the type of parents who always put family first. Being there for my sister and me through every age and stage of life was of utmost priority to them. And they chose to own their own businesses for the freedom and flexibility that brought our family.

My mom started an in-home daycare after my older sister was born so she could stay home, raise us, and be as involved as possible. After being a part of his family business for many years, my dad decided to launch his own business so he could create his own hours and show up for every sporting event and school music program. We always ate dinners together—often Mom's home-cooked meals.

This all seemed very normal to me as a kid. I didn't know any difference, given that my parents were both self-employed. As an adult, I realized that my sister and I, by following in our parents' footsteps, were inspiring entrepreneurs from a very early age.

Our top business endeavors were our annual summer carnival, our performances, and our good ol' nature museum. From dance shows to fashion shows to plays, we were quite the performers, and we loved casting the daycare kids in different roles. I can't imagine being the parents who had to watch them. For every performance, we charged a dollar for admission and fifty cents for popcorn. Then we'd pile our profits to buy a new, exciting toy.

We lived just outside town on a dead-end road with fields of corn behind our backyard—very Midwest. How in the world elementary school kids had the idea to start a nature museum in their backyard and charge adults to come look at sticks and rocks, pick some berries, and buy a souvenir is beyond me. Nevertheless, it was a hit!

As I look back, the funny thing is that I thought this was *normal* kids' stuff. It took me years to realize it was not. We were passionate entrepreneurs and entertainers, creating something from nothing and making a living doing it. Okay, I will say that we never had any expenses. Our parents never charged us for the supplies they bought, so it was purely profit. Nevertheless, we saw opportunities and went for it.

Maybe you weren't a little entrepreneur in your childhood—or maybe you were, and that's all the more reason you own or dream of owning a small business for yourself. But *we made the most of what we had*—whether that was pine cones or corn stalks—and continued to dream *big*.

That is what I love about small-town roots. Even if you weren't raised in a small town, you can grasp the concept of making the most of what life gives you. Just as the young entrepreneur takes lemons and turns them into lemonade, you can do the same! Work with what you have and just *start*.

You won't get anywhere unless you get over the fact that there will never be perfect conditions for starting out. It fascinates me how we don't care about being perfect when we are kids. We just create from what we have—like a nature museum of sticks and rocks—and are encouraged by it.

Somewhere along the way, though, we lose the confidence we had as kids to not be perfect. We begin to feel pressure from society to conform. Being normal becomes the goal. Not standing out but fitting in. We push down our playfulness in the name of being productive, keeping up, and always trying to be perfect.

Even as I grew up, I started to feel pressure from school and society to leave my small town and go to college to get a degree if I wanted to be successful and follow my big dreams. And chances are, if you're a small business owner, the traditional path probably didn't sit right with you either.

Yet there are so many advantages to dreaming big in a small town. You learn how to have a work ethic, have grit, and work with the hand you've been given. You may even fill a gap in your small town with a business idea. It's a prime opportunity to serve your community in a beautiful way while making a living for yourself and your family. So, don't dismiss the opportunity to build a business or follow a dream in a small town. It could be your biggest advantage for success as you work with what you have and turn your passion into your purpose.

Growth Lessons

There can be a stigma in your small town that somehow equates staying there with limiting yourself. But no matter where you come from, you can pursue big dreams in a small town—and staying in that small town can be your greatest advantage in creating success for yourself. Don't let others limit what you believe you can create for yourself. You decide your version of success, and it has nothing to do with the fancy degrees you have or where you live.

Even if you haven't had the support to dream big, you can probably think of an underdog story—someone with a less-than-ideal upbringing who decided to go for it no matter their circumstances, took the hand they were dealt, and made something of themselves.

I challenge you to let go of the assumption that you have to conform to society to be successful. Work with what you have. And don't let the dream killers and people around you who didn't go after their own dreams bring you down. If you're not sure what your big dreams might be, think back to what you loved to do as a child. We all had big dreams at one point before the world whispered to us what was and was not possible.

Embrace Your Inner Child

As a little kid, I was about as nerdy as you can imagine. I always had my nose in a book. I loved writing as much as I loved reading, and I used to pull out my grandparents' old typewriter and type up stories when we'd go and visit them. As I got older, my story writing turned to paper writing. I learned to love English class and developed a love for history. I was always top of my class, got perfect A's, was the president of the National Honor Society, and always prided myself on my academic accomplishments.

All this describes how nerdy I was and how nerdy I looked. In elementary school, I was this scrawny, lanky little girl with a short brown bob and glasses. Imagine Velma from Scooby-Doo—and yes, that's actually what I looked like. I got bullied for wearing my button-up sweaters, turtlenecks, and glasses and for trying hard in school. Yet, despite my nerdiness, I also acquired a love of playing softball and lifting weights.

While my sister became the hunter in our family, my thing with my dad was playing ball. We'd go out in the backyard and play catch for hours, and it was one of my favorite things in the world! But I was about the lankiest, scrawniest kid you'd ever seen. I had long arms and long legs with no muscle.

Second base became my position because I didn't have the arm to make the throw from third base or from shortstop to first, but I had a heck of a lot of heart and the drive to improve. I was serious about getting stronger so I could hit the ball farther and throw faster and farther. So I found the weight room in middle school. I started working out almost every day after school in the offseason so I'd be ready for spring softball, which carried into summer ball. I continued my lifting routine into high school and started to see my strength gains paying off.

I could see how my consistent daily lifting in the weight room all summer, during the season, and in the offseason led to me being the best softball player I could be. I became team captain, was at the top of the batting lineup for hitting the most doubles, and was the only one who played second base and became notorious for diving after anything. More than anything, though, I fell in love with fitness and learning to love the process.

As team captain, I felt it was my responsibility to motivate and inspire the team to hit the weight room with me, and I was most likely the most annoying teammate at five a.m.—bouncing around and getting everyone hyped up to lift when most of them would rather be still sleeping. (This was a skill I never knew would later serve me and become one of my superpowers!)

In fact, it's obvious to me now that all these childhood passions and pursuits led me to discover my super strengths that serve me as an adult.

I loved creating and performing like my sister and I did in our early years of entrepreneurship, when we created businesses and performed shows for anyone who would take the time to watch us. It gave me the courage to start my first business and lead a group of people—whether that was in my fitness and yoga classes or on stage in front of hundreds of small business owners.

I loved learning, reading, writing, and teaching, which is exactly what I spend most of my time doing these days. I study business concepts, then create content and share it through speaking engagements, my podcast, and this book.

I loved moving, playing sports, and leading a team to greatness—which is what I spent the first decade of my life doing. I led fitness and yoga classes, and now I lead small business owners to feel empowered!

Growth Lessons

Lean into what you loved to do as a child. Your original passions and personality can tell you a lot about how you'll find your path doing what you love as an adult. What did *you* love doing as a kid? Have you embraced that as an adult, or have you pushed it down further, trying to follow society's traditional path to success? Whether you are a business owner or not, how can you nurture your passions to create purpose in your work? My guess is if you *are* a business owner, your passion is what inspired you to start your business in the first place. Oftentimes, we lose ourselves as adults. So, go back to your passions and nurture your inner child. If you could do anything in your free time (yes, imagine you have some), what would light you up again?

Working Hard for What You Want (Sweat Equity)

I never got an allowance. Growing up, I was taught that if I want something, I have to work for it. As I approached high school, the idea of a car started popping into my head, and I knew that if I wanted to buy a car, I needed to create a plan.

At age fourteen, I applied for my first job at a pizza place in town. Since I was so young, all I could do was wash dishes and answer phones, which I was happy to start with! Eventually, I worked my way to serving and started saving up tips for my first car. I knew my parents wouldn't be able to afford a car for both my sister and me. And, in all honesty, I wanted my own.

A week before I turned sixteen, I had $3,000 in cash that I'd saved, and my dad helped me find my first car. It was a teal two-door Pontiac Sunfire, and, man, did it sparkle and shine. I was so dang proud of that car—and I know it was because I worked so hard for two years to save up for it. That car lasted me six years—well into college. It was my first taste of working hard for what I wanted, and I became addicted.

While most high schoolers were going to school, engaging in extracurriculars, and hanging out with friends every weekend, I was working and saving for my next big goal—college. At sixteen, I went to work for a local Mexican restaurant as a host and eventually worked my way to become a food runner, server, bartender, trainer, and, eventually, manager. By the age of eighteen, I was managing a restaurant. Looking back, it is wild to me that they trusted a young college student to manage a restaurant. But at the time, I didn't think anything of it. I worked my way up. Along the way, I came to learn every facet of the business other than cooking the food and somehow acquired leadership skills to train and manage other staff.

I worked at that restaurant for seven years—all through college— and made many friends and memories. I even met one of my absolute *best* friends to this day. We connected over work. We both had an insane work ethic and bonded over the experience of paying for our own college degree. Don't get me wrong—we had our fair share of fun nights out. But they came only after we closed the restaurant after a long double shift and had earned a pocket full of cash. Only once the work was done would we reward ourselves. We definitely knew how to have fun, but we worked our tails off to try and get ahead.

While some may have seen me as a little workaholic, I was simply motivated to make my way in the world by working hard for what I wanted and gaining life experience alongside it. Working with people of all ages and stages of life brought me so many relationships with people outside my typical peer group. It also brought me experience, wisdom, and many lifelong friendships that I would have never gained solely from extracurricular activities. I acquired skills, experience, and wisdom that would serve me greatly as I embarked on my journey into entrepreneurship.

If you are reading this book, you probably have also worked hard to get where you are. My guess is that your ambition began at a young age. When you look back on your first few job opportunities, what were some of the lessons you learned along the way? What gave you your first taste of working hard for a reward? Was it school, sports, or that first summer job? Chances are, it sparked a fire in you and a desire to go for more. That's the beauty of hard work: Even if it takes years, it is always rewarded.

Growth Lessons

Developing a strong work ethic and collecting life experience is essential for starting and scaling a business. If you have a desire to start a business, jump at opportunities to learn new skills, meet new people, and experience new challenges far before you start a business. They will come in handy more than you'd ever realize. If you've already launched your business, know that it often takes years to experience success. And be willing to put in the hard work, sweat, and sacrifice. True business success will never be found overnight or in a get-rich-quick scheme. Be willing to work for what you want.

There's another thing I came to realize about the traditional rules of society I mentioned at the beginning of this chapter (you know, go to college, get married, get a good-paying job, work until retirement, enjoy the last ten years of life, and be content). It's linear. And, as I'm sure you've realized, life is *not* linear. When you seek out your own path and learn to embrace the twists, the turns, and the path less traveled, it's simply more fun.

Whether you realize this at a young age or it takes you years to get there, know that societal messaging is strong and can still seep in, trying to influence you. Though I was a small-town girl from Wisconsin, I was still determined to dream big! I know now that following my passions led me down a path to finding my purpose. By working hard to reach my goals, I was collecting experiences and a work ethic that would serve me in my seasons of small business ownership.

But remember: Entrepreneurship is the path less traveled *because* it's hard. If it were easy, everyone would do it. You are on this journey because you are willing to put in the work. I was too, so I continued down the path less traveled—and something unexpected happened . . .

Chapter Reflections

Reflection Questions:

- ❖ What passions, hobbies, and talents did you enjoy growing up?
- ❖ How do they translate into what you're doing now or something new you could pursue?
- ❖ What past experiences, skills, and successes have you collected, and how can they serve you today?
- ❖ Where have you played small and limited yourself based on external circumstances?
- ❖ What is a dream you've been afraid to follow? What is stopping you?

Intentional Action:

- New Small Business Owner: Take that idea out of your head and put it on paper. Write down the skills, experiences, and relationships you have collected to help you bring your idea to life. Think of every idea possible to show why you should give it a go.
- Seasoned Small Business Owner: Try something *new* in your business or personal life. Take up a new class or hobby. Or sign up for a new experience, like attending a business conference. Go back to your roots and write down why you started your business in the first place. If that original spark of passion is not in your daily or weekly routine, how can you add it back in to get inspired again?

My first car I paid cash for (2008)

Chapter 2:

My First Child Is Born

Life-Changing Turning Points

Let me tell you a bit about my first child, who was born in June 2013. I was just twenty years old at the time and had the opportunity to birth my first baby: Zen and Pow Studio. If you've ever owned a business, you know exactly why I'm calling it my first child, especially before having actual children. Your business is your baby. And your first business is the one that is painfully close to your heart.

At the time, I was a twenty-year-old college student attending the University of Wisconsin-La Crosse to become a high school history teacher. I'd always been dead set on being a teacher. It's in my blood. But I didn't realize that I was going to fall in love with teaching fitness.

As you know, I grew up playing softball and enjoyed the weight room from middle to high school. But then I got to college and realized I missed working out with my team. I loved the energy and team dynamic that group sports and exercise cultivated. In my freshman year at the local tech college, I was required to take a class called Wellness Today. We did group workouts every week, and, while most people whined and complained their way through class, I loved every minute of it. No surprise there. I love a good challenge.

I especially loved the energy that my instructor, Nancy, brought to every workout. One of the days, we got to experience a cardio kickboxing class. I told her after class how it was my favorite workout we had done so far. She replied, "You know, you can get certified to teach this format!"

After doing a little digging, I discovered she was right. In fact, the local university was hosting an upcoming training called Turbo Kick. *No way*, I thought. This was the format of cardio kickboxing my sister and I had done at home together for years on our TV. Now I could get certified to teach a live format.

I decided to go for it. And that is what we call a *turning-point moment*—one of those moments we look back on later in life and wonder what our lives would have become if we hadn't done that *one* thing.

So I did that *one* thing. With the encouragement and nudge I needed from Nancy, I took that training—and that was the beginning of my group fitness journey.

I started teaching cardio kickboxing just once a week for fun at the local tech school where I attended classes my freshman year. But I wanted to teach people I knew from my hometown, about twenty minutes north of where I went to school. So I reached out to the local gym in town that had a basketball court that doubled as a group fitness room, and I struck my first business deal.

I started teaching just once a week. That turned into twice a week, and my classes continued to grow and grow. I was having a *blast*! Eventually, I decided to add a little Zen to my punches and kicks and enrolled in a two-hundred-hour yoga teacher training. I had always been intrigued by yoga. Growing up, I was the one middle school kid attending a yoga class at the local YMCA in a room of mostly older adults. This was way before yoga was cool, but I guess it was my old soul that became interested in not just the physical side of yoga but the yoga philosophy. So I invested in my growth and dove into my yoga teacher training.

After about two years of teaching and growing my Turbo Kick classes—and just as I was starting to dabble in teaching yoga—I got a phone call one day that completely changed my life. It was *another turning-point opportunity*. A local mixed martial arts (MMA) gym called Iron Works Training Center approached me. It was just down the road from where I held my weekly classes. They had heard great things about my classes (word travels fast in a small town) and were inviting me to rent their room upstairs. Essentially, it would be my own business.

While my classes were going great, what twenty-year-old doesn't want their *own* space and their own business? I knew this would be the perfect place to start teaching my yoga classes, then expand and see what I could do with this newfound instructing career I was creating and loving.

So I trusted my gut, seized the opportunity, and took the *leap*. *It turned out to be another turning-point moment.*

Growth Lessons

Be open to opportunities. You never know when something could be a major turning point toward your future! You may think you're on one path to achieve a goal when there could be an even better opportunity headed your way. Always be on the lookout for a way to align with the right opportunities at the right time—which is exactly what happened to me when I started my business.

As I look back, I have so much gratitude for the turning-point moments that birthed something so beautiful in my life just at the right time. Even when I was going through storms in my business, reminding myself of my why was so important in getting through the hardship.

If you're a business owner, I want you to look back on your "first child." Maybe it's the business you are currently running. Or maybe it's what got you into entrepreneurship in the first place and you've pivoted since. There is something so special about that first idea you took from seed to soil and grew, even if it is just a small sprout of a business. That's something! Many people will never take the leap to go for it with their ideas. So you should be proud of your courage to just start. If you're on the fence about an idea, maybe it's time to test the waters. No matter where you're at or how big your dream is, we all have to start somewhere. So I recommend starting small and growing slowly.

Start Small but Dream Big

Right before I opened my studio in June 2013, I had taken my annual summer solo trip out to visit family in Connecticut. But this trip was even more special because I got to dream big and they got to help me. My two aunts I went out to visit, and their families, have been in the fitness industry their entire lives and were so supportive and encouraging of my newfound venture and passion.

I sat around the table with them, trying to come up with a name for my new business. I knew I would start with yoga and kickboxing classes. Finally, we pieced together Zen and Pow! The best of both worlds.

I was still also working at the restaurant, and one of my co-workers there had just started graphic design school. So I reached out to her, and she helped me develop my first logo. The colors were teal and yellow, and the symbol was a yin and yang. It was perfect.

In June 2013, I opened up my studio doors for classes inside Iron Works Training Center, and the rest is history. It's been over ten years now since the birth of my first child—and, man, a lot has happened along the way.

But I just want to pause here to say that at the time, the decision to start teaching group exercise classes and launch my own studio felt so small and insignificant. I had no idea where this journey would lead me. So much of this book and my story happened because I followed small nudges along the way and was willing to start small, even when I had big dreams.

Looking back, I can see that I had zero clue what I was doing. But I somehow had the courage to try anyway. Even if it wasn't courage, it was all the encouragement I received along the way. I probably would have never gotten that first group fitness certification without encouragement from Nancy, who's now my friend. And I certainly wouldn't have started my studio at twenty without that call from Iron Works asking me to rent their space.

When you don't have the courage yourself, you may have to borrow it from those who believe in you before you believe in yourself. That has been a common thread along my journey.

And even when you feel unprepared, too young, or too inexperienced, there are small nudges along your journey that tell you to try anyway. You just have to be open to receiving them.

Like I said at the beginning of this chapter, I was on track to become a high school history teacher. And I somehow became a college student running a business. And dang, I was having *fun*! Being your own boss at twenty is pretty freaking awesome.

But there were a lot of tradeoffs too. Being a broke business owner *and* college student has a whole new meaning behind it. While most people my age were out partying every weekend, I spent my weekends working my butt off at that local Mexican restaurant I mentioned because I was paying my tuition, my rent, *and* my business expenses.

While I was constantly invited to go out for drinks every Thursday with friends, 99 percent of the time, I opted out because I taught yoga every Friday at five a.m. Although, I do recall a few times when I tried to go out. Let me tell you, teaching *hot* yoga at five a.m. on no sleep after a night of drinking is a punishment I don't wish on anybody.

While I always felt like a bit of an outlier—even in childhood and when I was growing up—being a business owner in college definitely exacerbated that feeling. I was so embarrassed of my business in the early years because I had such small, humble beginnings.

I didn't have any fancy equipment or a big marketing budget. In fact, it was quite the opposite. I was just a broke, bright-eyed, optimistic, quite naive (but it served me), and ambitious young entrepreneur following her dream.

The week before I opened my studio, I had a few of my restaurant co-workers help me hand paint murals on the walls, and the studio was essentially empty because I didn't have any money to buy equipment other than a few extra yoga mats. Turbo Kick and yoga were all I taught to start, which, thankfully, didn't require a ton of equipment—at least not at first. I didn't even have a point-of-sale system. I created punch cards from the local print shop, and people purchased them through Iron Works. Then the gym paid me every month for what was sold.

Eventually, I had a yoga student who loved what I was doing and offered to buy me some yoga blocks and bolsters. I gratefully took him up on the offer, knowing I couldn't afford it myself. But I knew having a few yoga props available would help me become more legitimate.

I chuckle just thinking about how little I knew about anything, let alone running a business in the beginning. I didn't have much, but I had all the passion, grit, and resiliency I needed, which carried me through and helped me make the hard decisions later in my journey. Starting small in a seven-hundred-square-foot room inside an MMA gym also gave me room to eventually grow into my big dreams.

Growth Lessons

I highly encourage business owners to start before they feel ready and without all the fancy stuff. The truth is, you don't need it to get started. When you have humble beginnings, you give yourself space to grow into your big dreams. If you start with everything you want from the beginning, you can rob yourself of the ability to learn as you go and to appreciate the small things and growth along your small business journey. We often are not ready to hold our big dreams right away anyway. Not to mention, you should prove that your business idea is going to work before you invest too much money and time into it. Give yourself room to learn, evolve, and grow without the pressure right away. One of my favorite mottos, especially for aspiring entrepreneurs, is "Start small but dream big!"

Getting Gritty to Get Started

Needless to say, going to school full-time, working nearly full-time at my restaurant job, teaching classes, and running my business was a grind. But I was *loving* it. After my first year at the local tech school, I transferred to the local university to complete my degree in education and finally become what I had set out to be—a high school history teacher.

I say I was born to be a teacher because I had desired that from a very young age. I was one of those kids who played school and loved coming up with class plans and activities. I even had a make-believe classroom in my basement. As I grew older, I realized that I could make a larger, positive impact on the world by teaching. I'd come to really enjoy history in school. So, naturally, that was the topic I wanted to teach. I had always loved old houses, lessons about the past, and historical fiction. And I wanted to share anything I learned with the world.

But it didn't take me long to realize that becoming a history teacher was no longer my dream. I had fallen in love with teaching fitness, and that was what was starting to excite me.

I had a conversation with my university counselor about getting into a classroom to do my student observations and student teaching. I was going to be a senior, and I hadn't stepped foot in a classroom yet. Because they had so many students and not enough placements, I was being denied that opportunity. Needless to say, the road to becoming a high school history teacher was definitely looking longer than four years. Oof.

My counselor knew I was getting discouraged and said, "Stephanie, you are so ready for this next step. I will vouch for you to get into a classroom."

It forced me to pause and think, *Is this really what I want to do? Can I even change my mind?* Because I'd definitely had a change of heart.

I told her I needed a day or so to think about what I wanted to do. And that was all it took to realize I didn't want to continue on the journey of becoming a high school history teacher. I wanted to continue on the journey of owning Zen and Pow. I wanted to see where my business would take me because the potential felt *unlimited* and so much more exciting than finishing school to become a history teacher for the rest of my life.

That pause was all I needed, and it was another turning point I will never forget.

But I am not a quitter—especially when I had already invested time, effort, and my own money into my college degree. So I figured out how I could pivot, graduate as soon as possible, and still acquire a degree without starting over. I graduated from the University of Wisconsin-La Crosse in December 2015, finishing in four and a half years with a bachelor of science degree with a major in history and a minor in nutrition.

Graduating college was a big deal to me not because of the fancy degree or the accolades or the fact that I stayed on the dean's list all through college. The real reason I stuck it out, even when I was completely mentally checked out, was that I was the first to graduate college in my family—and that alone made me proud.

When I graduated, family members said, "Congrats! What are you going to do with your degree? Where are you going to get a job?" I smiled back as I answered, "Nothing, actually. I don't need a job. I have a business." This statement still makes me smile and laugh. I'm sure they left that conversation horrified and wondering how the heck I was going to turn my part-time gig into a full-time career. But I was determined to prove anyone wrong.

After graduation, I told myself I was going to give this business one year to see what I could make of it. After graduating, I got gritty and pushed harder than ever. Now that I didn't have school to bog me down, I had even quit my restaurant jobs so I could dedicate all my time to my business—my baby. I increased my class offerings, started personal training, and picked up certifications in all different kinds of new formats to teach.

Being a tech-savvy millennial served me well as I started to utilize free platforms like Facebook and Instagram for marketing. Now, I'm aging myself here. But this was when social media was completely organic and there was no such thing as paid ads. Wild, I know! I was always taking photos of classes and posting about them on social media. That was how I built a strong organic following on these platforms. It seems obvious now, but back in 2013, not every business even had a website, let alone social media.

Speaking of websites, I started out with a basic Wix website—the kind that still had *Wix* in the domain name. Eventually, I wanted to appear more professional, so I bought myself a WordPress domain and hired a website designer to design the basic format for a few hundred bucks. Then I had her teach me how to keep it updated. I became a self-taught website designer and have since designed all my own websites on WordPress. I even started a YouTube channel of yoga and fitness videos that I filmed and uploaded so people could enjoy a taste of my classes online.

Needless to say, I was wearing all the hats: fitness instructor, yoga teacher, head of marketing and PR, bookkeeper (even though I was barely keeping books in the beginning), IT, janitor, and so many more. But hey, I learned every facet of my business. I was hoping that my hard work and grittiness would eventually pay off and I could hire someone to do the things I wasn't good at or didn't know how to do instead of spending hours teaching myself WordPress, email marketing, and bookkeeping. I was all about gaining experience to get ahead, and that took grit and the willingness to put myself out there, no matter how young, inexperienced, and dumb I often felt.

Whatever I could do to get free marketing and publicity about my business out in the world, I would do it. I can't tell you how many free classes I taught at the local schools, out in the community, and at local businesses over the years—probably hundreds. And while my time eventually became limited and I began to charge for these services, from the very beginning, I saw the value in these free offerings. If even one person had a positive experience and came to my studio or referred me to a friend, it was worth it. Plus, I thoroughly enjoyed leading classes and always loved getting to teach to a new, excited group of participants.

Another reason I got gritty was that I just didn't know what the future would bring. Why go all out on spending money I didn't have on a business that I wasn't sure would work out? I can't tell you how often I see new businesses make this huge mistake. So I bootstrapped it from the beginning. I borrowed equipment for kickboxing and personal training from Iron Works. I taught mostly body weight classes so I didn't need equipment other than some props and kettlebells until a few years in.

Within one year of graduating and getting gritty to get started, I had outgrown my seven-hundred-square-foot studio space. We were busting at the seams! And it was amazing. I had been at Iron Works for four years, and it had become my home. But I was feeling the nudge to go off and spread my wings. I could feel the next evolution of Zen and Pow and myself being birthed for something big and exciting.

Growth Lessons

Get gritty when you're getting started so you can build your business on little to no budget. Wear all the hats and learn all the roles. Eventually, you can hire and delegate, but learn every facet of your business so you know what you'll someday hire for. Develop your grit from the beginning and get comfortable being uncomfortable and putting yourself out there. Take every opportunity you have, especially in the beginning, to get in front of new audiences of potential clients. And yes, that often means doing it for free. We all have to start somewhere!

It was all because of the turning-point opportunities I took, even when it was uncomfortable. Even when I was unsure of myself. Even when I felt underestimated and embarrassed of my humble beginnings. Even when there were many opportunities for failure. Starting a business is the ultimate challenge to put yourself out there to be criticized, doubted, and misunderstood.

Speaking of putting yourself out there, how about stepping into a cage with thousands of people watching?

Chapter Reflections

Reflection Questions:

- ❖ What was a turning point in your own journey? How did it shape you?
- ❖ Where are you holding yourself back in your business because you feel like you are not ready or that it's not "perfect" yet?
- ❖ How can you take the start-small-dream-big mentality to either start a business, grow your business, or pivot and launch a new evolution of your business?
- ❖ What is a gritty marketing tactic you could try that wouldn't cost you anything but might require you to get uncomfortable and put yourself out there?

Intentional Action:

- New Small Business Owner: Test the waters on your idea. Dream big but start small—before you feel ready or decide that the idea is "perfect." Start beta testing and doing market research before you go all in on investing your time and money. Offer your product or service to a few friends, family, or people interested, then gather feedback. Know that you will never nail it on the first version of your product or service. Remember that we all start somewhere. Continue to evolve and adapt your business as you learn and grow!

- Seasoned Small Business Owner: First, be proud and celebrate yourself for your willingness to *start* your small business in the first place. If you're feeling stuck, go back to the basics of getting gritty. Maybe you need to get into the trenches again with your marketing and sales like you did in the beginning—building relationships and taking feedback. If you're looking to grow, take the same advice offered to the new small business owner and start small. Beta test your idea out in the world. Could you offer it for free or at an exclusive price to your top ideal clients, then gather their input? Take them along on the journey. Try a new marketing strategy without spending any money and get back to being gritty to grow into your next season.

Inside my first studio where Zen and Pow began (2013)

Chapter 3:

Setback Turned Comeback

Stepping Into the Cage

"You can't fight MMA . . . you're a girl!"

"Why would you want to ruin your face?"

I heard these words often when I decided to take on the ultimate challenge of fighting mixed martial arts.

During my first four years of Zen and Pow, being inside a mixed martial arts gym intrigued me. I became curious about training MMA. I'll skip the awful details, but let's just say I was coming out of a bad stretch of crappy boyfriends and horrible relationships. And you know the ones most girls experience at the end of high school and beginning of college? Yeah, I went through those too, and I wanted something to help me refocus on just me.

I'd always had an interest in boxing. In fact, I received a boxing bag and pink Everlast boxing gloves for Christmas in high school. But at the time, there wasn't anywhere to learn the skill or train.

I started staying after the classes I taught in my studio to take MMA classes to try it out. I tried it all—boxing, jiujitsu, and wrestling—but my favorite was Muay Thai, often known as kickboxing. I loved

Muay Thai because, at the time, I was still pretty scrawny. But, man, I could move. Footwork and finesse had been my strengths in softball growing up—paired with my go-for-it attitude to never give up.

As you know, I was never naturally strong in childhood. And even as a young adult, my long legs and arms were still just as lanky and scrawny. So, while my punches weren't exactly hard, could I ever kick and move! When I combined my natural flexibility with my ability to move my feet quickly, I could throw a head kick and get out fast.

Once I started training, I got the itch to compete—like most competitive people do. At the time, women's MMA was just beginning to spark interest, but it was still rare to see a girl fight. Well, I got this crazy idea in my head that I wanted to take a fight. As you now know, I love defying stereotypes, *and* I love a good challenge.

Iron Works ran a local MMA promotion that held fights twice a year. After attending a couple of their fights to cheer on gym friends and teammates, I thought, *Why can't I get in there and compete?* I knew it wouldn't be easy. But I also knew that if I put in the work, win or lose, it would be an experience that most would never have the courage to try.

The desire to go against the grain and challenge myself in a new way seems to draw me to new ideas and challenges. You know by now that I've never been a "follow the path that society wants you to" type of person. Doing something that most people would never have the guts to do and just seeing how far I can go is very exciting to me.

So, after watching my friends compete, I decided that I was going to take a fight in September. That gave me about four months of training, which I didn't realize at the time is not that long when it comes to learning many new skills. And that's the thing about training and fighting MMA: You can't be good at just one skill. You need to be well-versed in your stand-up, your ground game, and everything in between. That's because a fight can go either way. So I had to immerse myself in learning how to do submissions and chokes in jiujitsu, deliver punches and kick combos in boxing and kickboxing, and perform and block takedowns in wrestling.

That's *a lot* to learn and get good at in four months. My wiser self, who's writing this, is laughing, shaking her head, and thinking, *Oh, Steph!* It wasn't that I was cocky or overconfident in thinking I could learn all of this. It's just that when I set my mind to something, I am going to go all in and see it through. I don't want to wait around to do it. So, waiting a whole year to compete felt like an eternity. So yes, September it would be.

Once I committed, the comments rolled in:

"You can't fight. You're too nice!"

"Why would you want to ruin a pretty face?"

"Girls shouldn't be fighting MMA."

I politely smiled and thought, *If you think I can't or shouldn't do it, watch me!* These comments only put fuel to my fire. You shouldn't tell me not to do something you don't want me to do because I'll make it my mission to do the opposite and prove you wrong. Just ask my dad. He'll tell you.

Even though not everyone understood or supported my decision to fight MMA, my coaches, my teammates, and even my Zen and Pow clients were very supportive of me in this season. I made it official when I signed my fight contract and locked in my fight to compete in the 135-pound weight class for women.

I trained my tail off that summer to prepare for this fight. Luckily, I didn't have to cut a lot of weight for the fight. Unfortunately, my opponent did but decided not to. When the day of weigh-ins came—

the day before fight night—she weighed in around 145 pounds. That was almost a whole 10 pounds more than me! At that point, it was my decision to take the fight or not. Of course I was going to. I hadn't worked that hard to not compete.

Fight day came and, of course, I was nervous. But I was also very excited. We had not one but four girls from our gym fighting on the card, and we all trained together. It was exciting to cheer each other on. I watched them go first, which made me even more nervous. My fight was about halfway through the lineup, right before the pros. In an amateur fight, you fight for three minutes for three rounds. If someone doesn't get a TKO (a.k.a. knockout) or submission, or if the ref doesn't stop the fight for some reason, it will go all three rounds, and the judges will score it for the winner.

I went all out for this fight, including finding sponsors and making shirts. The shirts were bright neon yellow with one of my favorite quotes on them from Beau Taplin: "She was unstoppable not because she did not have failures or doubts, but because she continued on despite them." When it was time for my fight, I walked out, seeing nothing more than a blur of bright neon yellow all over the venue! I had sold a lot of tickets, and there were so many friends, family, and fans there to cheer me on.

My coaches in my corner greased me up with Vaseline and checked my mouth guard and gloves. Then I ran into the ring and heard *click, click* as the cage door shut and locked. *Holy crap, this is actually happening,* I thought. It's hard to explain the experience of your first fight. You have no idea what you're in for, and you're running on just pure adrenaline.

Okay, focus, I told myself. My opponent and I danced around a bit while standing. I took a few punches and threw a few back.

She had quite a bit of height and weight on me, so she took me down fast. My head got caught, and I took some punches on the ground. But I got my footing and stood back up, pushing her against the cage and throwing shots to her body. She took me down again, and I was fighting to not give up my back because that would have meant a rear naked choke—and that was exactly what happened.

Now, at this point, you are normally supposed to tap out so the ref can stop the fight before you go unconscious. Well, you know me enough by now to know I am not a quitter. I was still fighting back. While up against the cage, I was looking at one of my teammates, who was sitting right next to it. He looked horrified, as I'm sure he realized what was about to happen. My face went black and blue, then my body went limp . . . and I was out.

What came next was the worst part of the whole fight. I was lying unconscious on the mat when my very unclassy opponent got up and decided to make choking motions, mocking me. The crowd yelled, "*Boo!*" I finally awakened from my sixty-second slumber that I'm sure left most of my family and friends horrified. They were probably also determined to never watch me do this MMA thing ever again.

I was still out of it when the ref held both our hands and raised my opponent's. She went in to hug me and kiss my face as the crowd booed again. She wasn't winning anyone over at this point. My confused, half-awake self left the cage as the ref asked her, "Is there anything you want to say?"

She replied, "Thank you, Stephanie!" in the sassiest way.

If I hadn't been coming out of being unconscious, I wish I could have responded, "No, thank *you*. Thank you for teaching me to never be as classless as you and to be a good sport, win or lose. Thank you for putting a fire in my soul to train harder, be better, and not quit after my first loss. Thank you for showing me what it's like to put myself out there to fail and feel humiliated in front of thousands of people and still hold my head high and try again."

I'm sure this girl has no idea how this loss not only gave me the desire to try again in MMA but formed in me the mindset of resilience, persistence, and determination that I used in every area of my life going forward—especially my business.

I wanted to share this chapter of my MMA journey in this book because it is a daily reminder to me to be the type of person and business owner who is willing to put themselves out there, try, fail, get back up, and try again. My time spent fighting MMA is a constant reminder of my own resiliency and a reminder of this quote by Teddy Roosevelt:

It is not the critic who counts; not the man who points out how the strong man stumbles, or where the doer of deeds could have done them better. The credit belongs to the man who is actually in the arena, whose face is marred by dust and sweat and blood; who strives valiantly; who errs, who comes short again and again, because there is no effort without error and shortcoming; but who does actually strive to do the deeds; who knows great enthusiasms, the great devotions; who spends himself in a worthy cause; who at the best knows in the end the triumph of high achievement, and who at the worst, if he fails, at least fails while daring greatly, so that his place shall never be with those cold and timid souls who neither know victory nor defeat.

Growth Lessons

Starting a business is the ultimate form of putting yourself out there on a public platform and learning how to fail forward! Even if you fail in your business—which you will eventually—you at least did so while daring greatly. And that is better than never knowing victory or defeat. Most people are not willing to fail, let alone fail publicly, so they never try. Every successful person talks about having the willingness to fail and how they've had more failures than successes.

So, when was the last time you allowed yourself to fail? It doesn't need to be in an arena full of people. Maybe it was on the smallest scale. I love the saying "You'll never know unless you try" because it's the absolute truth.

If there's anything I've learned from business, MMA, and life, it's that the failures will shape you forever. You'll never forget them, the lessons you learn from them, and who you become because of your failures. I promise, the more you are willing to fail, the more success you'll find in business and in life.

So, what are you willing to try today that might be scary and overwhelming but that—win, lose, or fail—will make you better because you had the courage to do something new? You'll hear about many more of my failures in this book. I hope they're a reminder to you to keep showing up despite your fears and failures because they will become some of your greatest stories.

Separation Season

I've always hated running. It was my least favorite form of exercise. I'd rather be punching or kicking something. But once I was no longer training MMA, I started running at the age of thirty for a new physical and mental challenge.

One cold December day in Wisconsin, I did not want to run. But it was my running day of the week, and my mindset was that it was "separation season," which is the time of year when most people give up on goals they haven't hit yet and put off becoming the best version of themselves until the new year.

Therefore, it was my time to separate from the ordinary and average and challenge myself when most don't. It's how you can get ahead in most areas of your life. It doesn't mean I wasn't enjoying the holidays, relaxing, and reflecting. But it's a mindset that has kept me accountable to myself and the goals I've acquired during previous chapters of my life.

It's just like anything—once I got started running, I was feeling great. I challenged myself to run the farthest I ever had and push my pace. And dang, I wasn't even winded!

Then, out of nowhere, for probably the fifth time in the last decade, my left ankle just gave out. I fell, bloodied and bruised, on my opposite knee and had to limp, sad and frustrated, back to my car.

I'm kinda like a walking injury. My hypermobility has put me down and out more times than I can count, and it's always so frustrating—especially when I'm just trying to challenge and better myself. So I let myself have a little pity party on the couch at home for a bit and rest. But I reminded myself that this ankle sprain was just a minor setback. I've had plenty of setbacks over the years that I turned into comebacks.

Now that you know how I got into MMA and the story of my humiliating loss, I'll tell you how I came back from that loss. I focused on separating myself from my competition and used all my setbacks to inspire my comeback.

I decided to take the entire year to train after my first MMA loss before committing to fight again. My normal day looked like this:

- Get up at four a.m. to teach a Zen and Pow class at five a.m.
- Drive home and head to class at the university.
- Go home to do schoolwork.
- Drive back to the gym to teach more Zen and Pow classes at five and six p.m.
- Train MMA until nine or ten p.m.
- Make dinner and go to bed around eleven p.m.
- Get minimal rest and *repeat*.

It was insane how I lived during those years. Many days, I was teaching classes twice a day. I would even train MMA twice a day in the months leading up to fight camp. How did I sustain myself?

Crazy amounts of pre-workout and pots of coffee—literally. I won't go into my caffeine and pre-workout addiction, but just know this: You may think I love my coffee now, but I have come a lonngggg way since my caffeine addiction then.

It was decided that this fight card would be in August instead of September. *And* it was going to be outside at our local ball field stadium. How cool! I knew this was the one I had to compete in. I mean, after all, I grew up playing softball. I was just concerned about one thing: getting my dang hand raised for a win.

As I trained for this fight over the course of the year, I experienced many injuries. First, I dislocated both of my shoulders while landing on my elbow in wrestling practice. My shoulder blades popped in and out.

Not only am I naturally scrawny and lanky, but my joints are extremely hypermobile, which always made me "good at yoga"—which, I later learned, was *not* a good thing. In fact, because my elbows are so hypermobile, I would have to tell the ref before a fight that if he saw my elbow looking dislocated in an arm bar, to please not stop the fight. That was just my arm, as I have extreme range of motion.

Also, I am left-handed at three things:

1. Writing
2. Shooting pool
3. Kickboxing

As a southpaw, my left arm is supposed to be my power punch. But, after I dislocated my left shoulder multiple times in a few months, that was not the case. In fact, sometimes my shoulder would even pop out as I was throwing a punch.

So I learned to adapt and pivot—a recurring theme in my life, as you'll come to find out. I started switching stances a lot more often so I could move in and out and avoid using my left arm as much as possible. As I think back on that, it's weird. After I started focusing on strength training over the past few years, my left arm rarely bothers me now, and I feel stronger than ever. But during my MMA days, I didn't have half as much strength, and I was overtraining without enough recovery.

Not only did I lose power in my punching due to my injuries, but I dislocated my left ankle at least twice while training and sometimes while just walking. It's so unstable that, to this day, I will be just walking or running, and my ankles will give out—just like I described at the beginning of this chapter. So, strengthening my ankles, knees, and balance was a challenge I was constantly overcoming.

But these injuries were not going to slow me down in reaching my goal to get my hand raised in this fight. They were motivating me to keep going and prove my underdog story. As I look back on this time as my older and wiser self, it is clear that I wasn't getting the rest and recovery I needed to let my injuries fully heal. Therefore, they just kept happening. But being young, naive, and determined sometimes got the best of me.

I wrapped and taped my wobbly joints and kept on training and preparing for my fight on August 22. My mindset was as strong as ever, and I just couldn't wait to prove my skills and ability in the cage.

I was strength training for this fight because I knew I seriously needed to try to strengthen my muscles to help avoid further joint injuries. We were about a month out from fight night when I was lifting weights. I was feeling good and challenging myself when I cried out, "*Owwwwwww!* Noooo!" Then the tears came.

I'd accidentally dropped a twenty-five-pound plate as I was loading it off the bar, and it fell directly on my left big toe. I managed to finish the upper body workout, but by the time I got home and took my tennis shoes off, my entire foot had swollen up and my toe was bleeding.

I went to the emergency room and heard the dreaded words: "There is no way you're going to be able to fight in a month." At first, I took those words to heart and was crushed. I had trained so hard all year and improved so much. I didn't want to let this be the reason I couldn't compete.

So my mind was set. I had worked through and continued training despite all my other injuries. This was going to be the final setback for my comeback, and I thought, *Man, this will make an awesome story.*

So I controlled what I could. I took those first few days to let the pain and swelling subside, focused on nutrition, and got to work on my mindset. Not only was I now dealing with another physical obstacle, but MMA is very mental. The second you get in your head and doubt yourself could be your make-it-or-break-it moment. I knew that my mindset needed to compensate for whatever my physical body would be lacking. I needed to continue to separate myself from my competition by having a mental edge.

I wrote Post-it notes as daily reminders of my strength, then stuck them all over my bathroom mirror. I spent a lot of time visualizing exactly how I wanted the fight to go, which meant me being able to compete no matter the state of my broken big toe.

After a week or so of resting, it was time to get to work. I was about three weeks out and needed to keep up my cardio to lose five to ten pounds for weigh-ins. The dreaded Airdyne bike became my best friend. I did sprints on that awful machine to get my heart rate up without putting pressure on my foot because separation season!

Growth Lessons

To find success in any sport, life, or, especially, business, you need to build your ability to work hard and separate yourself from the average, the ordinary, and your competition—especially when it's hard and you don't want to. You need to not only separate yourself mentally but also find your business differentiators. What makes your brand different from your competitors? How can you lean into what makes your business unique and capitalize on it more?

Holding this mindset of separation season has helped me in business when it would have been easier to coast, take my foot off the brake, or even quit. Instead, I'd try to find an advantage, which often comes down to building a mindset of resilience.

Finding Your Inner Fighter

One week out from fight night, I still couldn't walk normally, but I was feeling pretty dang good. I'm sure my family, friends, and clients thought I was crazy for still wanting to compete, but my teammates and coaches were supportive. I think that by this point, most people had just accepted that I was going to do what I wanted to do anyway. Remember, I'm stubborn! So it was pointless to try to convince me otherwise.

The weight cut is always the fight before the fight, and although most women don't cut as much weight as men, losing an additional 5 pounds is pretty hard for women. That was especially true for me when I was already sucked in. I decided to fight at 125 pounds for this fight, so losing those last few pounds wasn't easy. I would sweat in my studio as I turned the heaters on. Then, the night before weigh-ins, I'd just stop eating until after I'd weighed in the next day. Totally unhealthy, by the way. This is the part of the MMA world that I hate.

This time, I was fighting an opponent my teammate had fought and beaten on the previous show. So we were both 0–1 and very hungry for a win. But I knew that, with all my injuries and my first humiliating loss, I was hungrier. I wasn't going to leave that cage without my hand raised for a win!

The day finally came, and I still wasn't walking completely normal. But I did everything I could to not show my opponent I was injured. She had no idea I had dislocated my shoulder, sprained my ankle, and broken my big toe—all on my left side. Those would have been easy targets for her to take advantage of.

My walkout song came on—"Hells Bells" by AC/DC—which still makes my heart pound to this day. I made the walk from the outfield to the cage, staring down my opponent the entire way. I was in the zone and ready to get this fight over. I had nerves, but nothing like the first fight. It's amazing how much more confidence and excitement I had this time around.

My corners greased me up with Vaseline and checked my mouth guard and gloves. Then I ran into the ring. *Click, click.* The cage door shut and locked. This time, I was more than ready.

We danced around the cage a bit, as I'm more of a counter-puncher before I get aggressive. Once we started exchanging punches, we were getting into it on our feet. Despite my foot, I am a kickboxer, so I was more comfortable staying standing anyway. Plus, I was afraid that if we went down, my shoulder might dislocate once I hit the ground.

The rounds were the same as my first fight—three, three-minute rounds. And in this fight, we were able to throw knees to the body as amateurs. You best believe I took full advantage. I heard the *tap, tap*, which meant there were ten seconds left in the round. Then came the horn. The first round was done. *Yes!* I had made it through the first round, and I was just getting warmed up.

My corners told me to keep it up, stay on her, and keep moving in and out—don't take so many punches. Yeah, fewer punches to my head was a good idea, even if they weren't hurting me, I suppose.

Round 2 began. I could hear my corners yelling combos at me, which made it fun. I wasn't in a weird fog of adrenaline like I'd been in during my first fight. I was doing well, and I could feel the momentum building. I'm not sure who won that second round. But I heard the *tap, tap* and the horn. Then I went back to my corner. I had one more round to prove I deserved this win.

Round 3, here we go. I always get better as I go, as I need to warm up to things, no matter what I'm doing. So, by Round 3, I was feeling good. I was more aggressive in going after my punches and making my opponent move.

Jab, head kick. Cross, head kick. I was landing my combos solid, and I could hear the crowd getting loud as I did. My corners were yelling at me to stay on the offense, meaning to keep going after her and not let up.

At this point, she was sick of taking my punches and kicks, so she pinned me against the cage. Crap, I'd been there in my last fight, and it didn't end well. *This is why I worked so much takedown defense*, I thought. *Don't you dare let her take you down to the ground.* My corners were yelling, "Steph, underhook!" So I got the underhook and spun her around to pin her up against the cage instead. I threw more knees to her body as we were both fighting for control.

I heard the *tap, tap* again and knew I had ten seconds to finish this fight and get the *W*, even if it went to a decision. The horn blew, and I put my hands up to signal that I felt I'd won. But in all honesty, I was just catching my breath. I headed back to my corner while the judges made their decision.

The ref called us back to the center and took both our hands. The announcer said, "Ladies and gentlemen, our judges' scorecards are in. Judge number one scores 29–28 for Stephanie Helmers."

The crowd cheered, and my heart started pounding. That was one for me. "Judge number two scores 29–28 for Hannah Singer." The crowd cheered, and my heart pounded harder. This was a split decision.

"Judge number three scores 29–28 in favor of your winner by split decision, Stephanie Hellraiser Helmers!"

And finally, my hand went up in the air for that win.

You could have seen on my face how much that hand raise meant to me, as I started to get teary-eyed. Most people in the crowd probably had no idea why that win meant so much. It wasn't just about the win. It was about everything leading up to it. It was about having to find my inner fighter.

I'd overcome the fear of challenging myself to learn a new sport and many new skills as an adult.

I'd come back after an extremely humiliating first loss, after which it would have been easier to hang up my gloves right then and there and never try again.

I'd fought through injury after injury up until fight night.

I'd proven that a broken toe wasn't going to keep me from accomplishing my goal of a win.

I'd proven to myself that I was a fighter—not just physically but in my heart and soul. I will always fight to be the best version of myself and never give up when life throws me obstacles.

My opponent was a class act and hugged and congratulated me on a great fight. What a difference from that first fight. Just the sportsmanship alone was a huge win because my opponent was so kind and respectful. We even won the Fight of the Night award—something I'll cherish forever. I limped the rest of the evening, as my foot was sore, but it was more than worth it.

That was one of the best nights and proudest moments of my life because I truly felt like a fighter. In the chapters to come, you'll see how often I've utilized this fighter mentality and my underdog comeback story to push myself to keep going when life and business get hard and I want to quit.

While I wanted to keep training and fighting after this big win, I eventually had to choose between my business and fighting. As you can probably imagine, MMA is hard on your body. And as much as I loved it and trained for fun following this fight, the injuries were never-ending for me. Every injury meant time I couldn't teach my classes, and that was just no longer an option as I grew and scaled my business.

Growth Lessons

Find ways to build your mindset of resilience for entrepreneurship. Mine has come from MMA, running, and working out. You can separate yourself from your competition and learn to tap into your fighter mentality when you're challenged. Entrepreneurship will test you mentally more than you even realize. So, figure out how you can discover your own inner fighter when you're in a valley and you need it.

In what ways are you stepping into the arena in your own life and business and being willing to put in the blood, sweat, and tears—even if it means failure? How can you separate yourself from your competition and turn your challenges and failures into opportunities and advantages? Taking a setback and turning it into your comeback is one of the best skills you can acquire as an entrepreneur. But you'll discover it only if you're willing to embrace the journey and tap into your own fighter mentality.

Through my MMA experiences, I realized that it had never been about the *win*. It was everything leading up to it that made me who I am. It was the fight before the fight—the determination to continue when so many people said I shouldn't.

So, what is *your* version of stepping into the arena, your separation season, and your setback turned comeback? How can you use it to your advantage? How can you tap into your inner fighter mentality when the growing seasons and the weathering-the-storm seasons make your harvest feel far away? If I can do it, you can do it. I know you'll benefit from drawing from your failures and tough seasons the strength you'll need in future seasons.

Be grateful for the early challenges in business and in life that you've overcome. They'll help you build the mindset of resilience. You'll appreciate being able to tap into this mentality during the inevitable seasons of growth and storm weathering that you'll go through on your small business journey!

Chapter Reflections

Reflection Questions:

❖ What is something that felt like a failure but that, in hindsight, was actually you failing forward? Meaning it led you to learn lessons and gain newfound strength.

❖ Is there an opportunity you are avoiding because you are afraid of failure, loss, or disappointment?

❖ How can you separate yourself from others in your industry to stand out? What are your differentiators?

❖ What past challenges have you overcome and turned into opportunities?

❖ How do you strengthen your own mindset of resilience for entrepreneurship? What activities allow you to tap into your inner fighter when business gets hard?

Intentional Action:

• New Small Business Owner: Acknowledge that the first step into small business ownership is to just start. And it's incredibly scary and hard. But if it was easy, everyone would do it. Discover and write down your advantages and differentiators. Ask your clients even, and then sing them from the rooftop in your marketing and the ways you talk about your business. Know there will be many challenges and uncomfortable moments. You must find a way to continue to build your muscle of resilience, whether that's in fitness, meditation, journaling, or whatever will help you grow stronger to be able to take on the hardships of entrepreneurship.

- Seasoned Small Business Owner: You're seasoned because you have most likely overcome many challenges already. Write down your top three hardest moments in business, how you overcame them, and what you learned. Post them somewhere you will see them often as a reminder. Then share your stories with others who need a boost of inspiration! Continue to seek out activities that strengthen your inner fighter and tap into your muscle of resilience. Invite other entrepreneurs to join you. They will need it at some point in their journey as well.

Getting my hand raised after I won my fight (2015)

Small Business Sister Story: Asia Parkhurst-Jacobs

Planting Seeds of Resilience

I've always known I wanted to own my own business. Even as a kid, I had big dreams of building something of my own. But after high school, I did what I was "supposed" to do—took the traditional path, hoping I'd figure it out along the way. Truth is, I had no idea what I wanted to do. That feeling of uncertainty weighed on me until I stumbled into my first opportunity as a small business owner: co-owning a dance studio.

The moment I stepped into that role, something clicked. I fell in love with the freedom and creativity, watching something grow from nothing. But as much as I loved it, I knew deep down I wanted to build something that was truly mine. So I made the tough decision to sell my half of the business, even though I had no clue what would come next.

Then, I met Steph. At the time, I was dabbling with the idea of starting a cosmetic line, unsure if it was the right direction. But through Sister Circle, I found a community that not only supported my vision but helped Small Town Beauty by Asia grow faster than I expected. Steph has been such a big part of my journey—always in my corner, always cheering me on, and now, you'll never catch her without a Small Town Beauty by Asia lip gloss in her pocket!

Owning my brand—putting my name on something and believing in it—has changed me in ways I never saw coming. It has pushed me, challenged me, and made me grow not just as a business owner but as a person. And if I've learned anything, it's that even the smallest seed can turn into something bigger than you imagined.

But Small Town Beauty by Asia isn't just about cosmetics. It's about helping people feel beautiful, connected, and seen. It's about proving that small-town dreams are just as powerful as big-city ambitions. More than that, it's about community. I'm passionate about small businesses and collaboration because I believe there's room for all of us at the top. We don't have to push people out of the way—we can lift each other up and rise together. That's what makes this journey even more fulfilling.

When we support each other, we all grow. That's what being a soul-preneur is about: building something meaningful while lifting others up along the way.

If I could go back and tell my younger self anything, I'd say:

"Every season of uncertainty, every moment of doubt, every unexpected twist will lead you right where you are supposed to be. So get ready to grow and weather any storms."

Because everything that once felt like an obstacle was actually guiding me to where I was meant to be. And I wouldn't trade it for anything.

Small Business Sister Story: Sarah Murphy

Seeds of Creativity: How My Past Grew into My Dream Business

I think that if you reflect long enough and you are truly aligned with what you are supposed to be doing, whether that be personally or in business, there is this illuminated path you can see of how you got there.

Looking back at my childhood or the experiences I had in high school, college, or the creative outlets I was drawn to, it's no surprise that I launched a niche business that helps small business owners market their businesses or brands in a digital capacity. I really do think that it is an amalgamation of all your experiences and the way that people around you "lend you courage" and help motivate you in ways you couldn't have done alone.

I was always a very creative kid, and thankfully my parents encouraged it. I was the kid who came to school with a papier-mâché and clay beehive and caught double takes walking into the class because everyone had thought I brought in a real one. You could almost always catch me capturing photos, burning CD playlists, or creating videos of anything and everything.

All these small but impactful moments had given my childhood excitement a real framework in my business. When I joined a women's small business community, Sister Circle, a few years back, I hadn't yet left my job or even launched my business yet. But the spark of the idea was there, and this community welcomed me with open arms. The more I continued to show up for the monthly meetings, the more I felt this pull to put these pieces together and create a business that would not only create a spark in me but help illuminate others' sparks for their business and passions as well.

Stephanie played an instrumental role in the birth of my business, Social Cues. She lent me the courage I needed to realize that with a little hard work and grit, the right room of people, and no fear to start small and dream big, my ideal business had been right in front of me all along! Through all my childhood creative endeavors and early life experiences, my business was there for the taking! And that was just the start of a turning point moment, and I can't wait to see where the passion for helping other small business owners will help me grow in life and business!

Part 2: Growing

"A garden is a grand teacher. It teaches patience and careful watchfulness; it teaches industry and thrift; above all, it teaches entire trust."

— *Gertrude Jekyll*

Chapter 4:

Leaning Into Your Intuition to Take Yourself to the Next Level

Taking Big Leaps in Business

You know when you just *feel* ready for the next thing? Whether I was actually ready for the next big growth leap in my business is questionable, but I felt ready! I was young and naive, yet I was also full of passion for this dream I was building. After four years of growing my business within the MMA gym, I was finally ready for the next big leap into my own space.

This is about the time when I started to really tune into my intuition in making business decisions and I paid attention to signs however they came to me. About one year after graduating college, pouring my heart and soul into my business, and having full classes, I felt the nudge to start to seek out my own studio space. I also started to notice the string lights and lamps in my studio flickering during yoga classes. At first I thought I was seeing things, but my members noticed it too.

I looked up the spiritual meaning of flickering lights and learned they are often a sign that angels are looking over you or there's an energy shift in your environment—which totally made sense in this case. I took it as a positive sign that I was on the right path. I could feel that something more was in store for me, and while it was scary and overwhelming to think about the next chapter, I was so excited to see what the future held for my dreams.

At the time, it felt like the hardest decision I ever had to make. Iron Works was my home. They gave me my first shot, believed in me, and supported me. And although I knew I had outgrown the space, I was sad to leave. I was crying when I walked into the office to deliver the news because I felt so bad to be leaving the first place I'd called home for my business. After having a painfully hard conversation with the owners of the gym, it was time.

Once the hard decision to find my own space was made, the lights stopped flickering and the excitement began!

At this point, I was only twenty-four years old, and the only thing I owned was my blue Chevy Impala. So, when I decided to leave, I knew I was going to need to take out my first business loan to do a build-out. That's the thing about certain industries, like the gym and yoga studio industry: It's pretty rare to find a space that is perfectly suited to your needs. You almost always need to put money into a build-out to make it what you need it to be. Not to mention equipment. I had been mostly teaching bodyweight classes with a few kettlebells and resistance bands I had purchased and borrowed from Iron Works. Other than that, I didn't have any equipment of my own. So my list of items and expenses was adding up quickly.

I finally found what I felt was the perfect space—just five minutes away from my original studio and a little closer to the larger city than my hometown. My dad came with me to help negotiate my lease.

I was fortunate enough to have parents who believed in me and were willing to sign behind me on my first business loan. That was my first big leap!

This location had triple the amount of space I'd had at my original seven-hundred-square-foot studio, but it was one big, open, empty room. So, in the build-out process, I got to design the space and split it into two separate studio rooms—one for yoga and one for fitness—plus a front desk space and even my own office! Then, once we started doing the build-out, it was brought to my attention that the space next to my studio rooms was vacant as well. My landlord offered me a deal to add it on. I realized I wouldn't have any space to put my gym equipment in the fitness room, so we decided to make that a twenty-four-seven gym that members could access with a key card. I called it Zen Power.

As a twenty-four-year-old, owning my own fitness and yoga studio and a twenty-four-seven gym felt like a dream come true. It was what I had dreamt of when I originally started my studio. Now I had the opportunity to create it before my very own eyes and see it come to life.

This was everything I had dreamt of. My business was growing and expanding. Little did I know, though, that this meant growing pains. You may be at this point in your business right now, where you're starting to take larger risks and bigger leaps. And although it's exciting, it's simultaneously terrifying. The idea of failure and the weight of responsibility start to creep into your mind. If you've grown and scaled a business, you definitely know this feeling.

Having my first loan felt overwhelming and scary. I knew I had to increase membership to make ends meet and get ahead, and I was working hard to do it. In this space, we could double our class options since we had not one but two studio classes going on at once. But that also meant doubling payroll.

I knew that by moving spaces and taking this big leap, I could no longer teach every class. During the first few years in my original space, I'd had a few instructors cover every once in a while or teach one class a week so I could have a night off. In order to keep up with what our members wanted and continue to grow in the new studio, though, we began to offer classes every single day. Monday through Saturday, we even offered multiple classes per day, and even two at a time, since we had the space. Obviously, this was impossible to do myself, and I was ready to grow my team.

It wasn't easy to choose the right people to train and essentially become an extension of me and the brand I was building. I lucked out with most of my team. But over the years, I also had my fair share of people who hired on to learn but then saw what I was building and tried to steal my members and start something for themselves. So, if you've ever been hesitant to bring someone into your business and teach them everything you know, I get why! Some people are there to support you and grow the business, and some people are there for themselves. Trust your gut, just like always, but know that you won't get it right every time.

There are usually signs, but we often don't want to see them. Either you want to believe someone is good for your business or you're hiring in a desperate situation. I've done both. Give yourself some grace. You are human. Hiring and firing is probably the hardest part of growing a team that no one prepares you for as a small business owner.

When I think back to all the best staff I ever had over the years, though, they were always people who started as members and wanted to become instructors, or they were interns who came into the business to learn and ended up sticking around because they loved it so much. When you make your first hire, it doesn't seem like much. But all of a sudden, you are a boss, even if you don't see yourself as such. You slowly hire another, and soon enough, you are unexpectedly a leader!

This is what happened to me. I slowly grew a team and suddenly had all of this responsibility not just for my members but also for my staff. I trained them on the basics of opening and closing the studio, using our software and equipment, and—of course most important—leading a class!

In the transition from my first studio to my second, we grew our team to six and were having so much fun adding new classes (like barre), new equipment (like TRX), and new members to always keep things fun and exciting. I was only twenty-four at the time, so everyone on my team was older than me. But things were going well, and I was slowly getting the hang of leading my team. While I could grit and scrape by for myself no problem, I began to feel the responsibility of leading my team amidst the new challenges this space was bringing me.

Growth Lessons

We often assume that business gets easier as we grow and scale, but it doesn't. Our challenges actually get harder. The good news is that we get smarter and wiser. New levels—like having your own brick-and-mortar, taking on debt in your business, or hiring and training team members—can bring next-level challenges that you are unprepared for. But that's the growth—and it's nothing you can't handle.

Many business owners avoid taking big leaps and scaling altogether because they're terrified of the new challenges it will bring. I encourage you to look at your leaps and growing pains as a good thing that will bring many new opportunities to learn what you do and don't want from your business. These growing pains will give you the insight to follow the right path for you, which always comes along with trusting your gut.

Trusting Your Gut

The first year of being in this studio space was a whirlwind of the honeymoon phase. I was high on life and passionate about what I was doing and what I was building. We had created so many new offerings in this space that were unique to our area, like barre, TRX, and kickboxing. Even my yoga classes had evolved from hot yoga to a more functional flow practice.

But after the first year or so, things started to feel heavy. Not only was it getting tough to acquire new members—since our location was far off the main roads—but the costs of so many things started to increase. Out of nowhere, my landlord started trying to control the temperature and lights in my space. Soon enough, I was coming into a fifty-degree gym space in the winter and having motion lights going off and on during yoga class.

It was like he flipped a switch and became increasingly difficult to deal with. The toilets started backing up, and my clients and I became his targets. He accused us of flushing wads of toilet paper and tampons down the toilet. One day, I came in to find signs inside all the bathroom stalls that had a laundry list of ridiculous things that were *not* to be flushed down the toilet, like rubber gloves, aquarium rocks, and needles. Needless to say, I was very confused and frustrated.

Up until this point, I'd not had a single issue with my landlord. In fact, I thought we got along great. Then, out of the blue one day, he told me that I now needed to pay my own utilities—which were supposed to be included in my lease. While I was already struggling financially, I didn't want to give up this space that I had just poured so much money into. So, in trying to be reasonable, I reached out to see if we could just have a conversation face-to-face to resolve the issue. I wanted to share with him that I was more than willing to pay my own utilities if I could sign a longer lease, as my original one was for only two years—another big mistake I'd made.

I got the biggest red flag when he replied that he would now communicate with me only via email and that he would be sending me a new lease to sign in the coming months.

My gut started to scream at me that this was a huge red flag and the writing was on the wall. He was going to wait a few months to send me a new lease so I had no time to find a new space. Then he'd jack up my rent and make me pay utilities. Basically, he was going to put me in a no-win situation for myself.

And while I wasn't the smartest twenty-five-year-old, I also wasn't dumb. And I *always* listen to my gut.

I was angry, upset, and frustrated at the situation. This was my *dream* space, and I'd thought I was going to be there for years to come.

What could I do? Well, I could start searching again. "This or something better . . ." I continued to tell myself.

I felt that same nudge in my heart that I felt when I left Iron Works. And once again, my yoga string lights started flickering. . . .

It was my sign that the energy had shifted once again and it was time to move onto the next chapter. It was scary yet exciting . . . time to take the next big leap. Little did I know that the next big leap would be *ginormous*!

I started to put feelers out for open commercial spaces. And this time, I didn't want something that was supposed to be an office space. I wanted something that was meant for a studio . . . and that's exactly what I found.

A couple people sent me a listing for a completely unfinished vacant space that was built perfectly for what I needed. The location was prime. It was a brand new state-of-the-art building created by the biggest dance studio in town—Misty's Dance Unlimited. Up until this point, I hadn't known much about the dance studio. I had heard about it growing up because I had dreamt of taking dance classes as a child, but I'd never gotten to experience it. More or less, I wanted to meet the woman behind the mission.

I scheduled a showing at the space and went to see it with my dad and sister. I knew the moment I walked in: *This is it.*

It had high ceilings and tons of natural light, and it was a blank canvas. I'm talking no drywall, no electric, no plumbing, no flooring— nothing. This space was completely unfinished. While I saw potential, my dad saw dollar signs, and he wasn't wrong.

My dad is a risk-taker like me. But he is also a realist and a concerned parent who just didn't want me to make big mistakes in growing this business, like I'm sure he did in his early years as well. He told me this space was too expensive and that I could not afford it. And I'm sure every other business that looked at it before I did thought the same thing. It was definitely way outside my budget.

But I saw that moving into this space meant I could meet Misty herself. And maybe, just maybe, I could learn a thing or two from her. To me, that would be priceless. Up until this point, I had yet to find a woman in business in my industry willing to help me, guide me, mentor me, and be real with me about her own journey. While the dance industry is different from mine, the business model is similar enough that I could translate much of what she had built into my own business.

So, after many meetings with my parents, my banker, and the attorney I had to hire—thanks to my landlord—I was told multiple times that this space didn't make any sense for me. The attorney specifically said, "This doesn't make any sense. Why not just stick it out with your landlord?"

Gosh, he had no clue what I was dealing with.

The unanimous opinion was that I should find a cheaper location and *not* move into this space that would require me to take on an even larger business loan to make it move-in ready.

But, if you've gathered any insight into who I am so far, you know that I didn't care what they said. I was going to prove them wrong.

Through all the discussions and negativity I faced moving into the space, I have to thank my sister for supporting me in this leap of faith. She told my parents, "Steph needs this space, and she needs a mentor. I know it's a lot, but she can do it." I'm so grateful to have a big sis who has always believed in me, even when I had a hard time expressing my vision. She has supported me through all my ups and downs—not just in business but in life. I'm grateful to her for always believing in me and supporting me, even when my ideas come off as a little out there and crazy.

Thankfully, even though I went against their advice, my parents still supported me. They really are the best. But they didn't just sign behind my loan like the last time. They had to back this loan with their own house. Not to mention, this loan was five times the amount of my original loan just two years earlier. And, man, I have to say that at twenty-six, I didn't fully grasp the amount of responsibility I'd just taken on.

But I was excited! I'd just experienced two years of big leaps, expansion, and growth like never before, and it was a thrill. But before I dive into describing this new space and all the new opportunities and experiences I gained through it, I first have to tell you about the chapter I always said I would write—because it was something I never thought I would experience . . .

Growth Lessons

Trust your gut and know when to pivot. You know when something or someone feels like a red flag. Do *not* ignore these vital signs. Even if you can't see the reason right away, you'll understand in hindsight where your intuition was leading you. Sometimes, they're green lights and good nudges that push you to your next level; other times, they're red flags that force you to get uncomfortable. Either way, your gut intuition will always lead you to your next level of learning, which ultimately comes with making beginner business mistakes and growing pains.

Chapter Reflections

Reflection Questions:

- ❖ What is a big leap you have taken in your business or life? How did it lead you to where you are now?
- ❖ Do you know how your intuition speaks to you? Is it through signs, a nudge in your gut, or repeating numbers?
- ❖ Think of an experience in which you saw red flags. What were they trying to teach you?
- ❖ Think of an experience in which you saw green lights. When did things just start to flow and doors flew open?
- ❖ Where are you avoiding a big leap in your business and why? What's holding you back?

Intentional Action:

- New Small Business Owner: The first leap into entrepreneurship is a *big* one! It can be scary and overwhelming yet exhilarating at the same time. If you haven't taken the leap yet, journal about what is stopping you. Where are you holding yourself back? If you've launched your business, learn to listen to your red flags and green lights as you grow along your entrepreneurial journey. Pay attention to how your intuition shows up for you and protects you. While it may not save you from a painful experience, it will guide you to the wisdom you're supposed to gain along the way.

- Seasoned Small Business Owner: You've probably experienced your fair share of red flags and green lights at this point and have gained lots of lessons and wisdom along the way. Because of this, you may even be questioning your next big leap because of some painful growing pains or negative experiences you have faced. You may question yourself when it's time to dream and take big leaps again if, in the past, your intuition led you down what seemed to be the wrong way. Trust your gut. It was never the wrong path when you showed up for the growth lessons, then gained wisdom and experience while learning about yourself along the way. Know that you are taking your next big leap from a place of strength, wisdom, and experience that you couldn't access prior. When you know better, you'll make smarter decisions. Build your trust back with yourself by following small nudges, tuning in, and collecting more wins until you're ready to trust that big leap again!

Grand Opening of my second studio location with my parents, sister, grandparents, and Ben (2017)

Chapter 5:

Growing Pains

Beginner Business Mistakes

If there's one chapter of my book that I always said I'd write, this is the one. Why? Because It was probably the most unexpected turn of events I never could have predicted. I thought that when I finally told my landlord I would be leaving the space, that would be the end of it. Little did I know that it was just the beginning of a long road of challenges ahead.

Let me preface this by saying that when I talk about myself being naive, I was. How could I not be? I was a young, passionate twentysomething-year-old just trying to make her mark on the world and inspire others along the way. When I moved out of Iron Works, I was coming from a place that felt like family. I don't think I ever even signed a formal lease, so this was all new to me.

When it came time to negotiate the lease for my second studio space, my dad came along to help me. We negotiated some things verbally, like how I wouldn't officially start paying rent until my build-out was done and my business was open and making money. I also assumed that when the two-year lease was up, I'd simply renew it like

I had done with all my apartment leases up until this point. As long as I was a great tenant, why would that even be an issue?

This was one of my first big beginner mistakes: not getting it in writing! It can be as simple as having something you agree on written down on a piece of paper and signed by both parties. You don't need to hire a lawyer for everything, although I do now have a lawyer I work with so that I'm always covering myself and my business to avoid any future legal mistakes. Just remember that in today's business world, you need to have any negotiation recorded somewhere on paper.

Ultimately, my mindset was that if I'm a kind person, solid tenant, and responsible business owner, nothing bad would happen to me. I was already constantly having to prove that I knew what the heck I was doing as a young entrepreneur, so I was determined to show my landlord how great a tenant and respectable a business owner I would be.

Beginner business mistake number two: thinking I could people-please my way out of any situation. I figured if I was likable and a good tenant, no one would ever intentionally try to hurt me or my business. Yet we often have no idea what someone else's intentions are or why they do what they do. You ultimately cannot control their actions. You can only control your own mindset, your own actions, and how you show up in the world. Learning to let go of how others' actions affect you negatively is extremely difficult and infuriating. Don't let it get the best of you.

And that leads to beginner business mistake number three: trusting someone who ultimately disappoints you and beating yourself up about it. You didn't know, and now you do. It's as simple as that. If you're anything like me, you try to see the good in people, which can sometimes feel like a weakness that people can take advantage of.

It's disheartening when you put your trust in someone only to have them show you why you shouldn't have—like I did with my landlord when I negotiated my lease. In situations of distrust, maybe you question yourself and your ability to make smart decisions. It can leave you feeling vulnerable and downright dumb. It can even push you into closing your heart down and becoming cold and jaded. But we all know that person who just assumes the worst of everyone. Sure, they might not get mistreated. But because they don't trust a soul, their small business journey is horribly lonesome. Don't be like them.

As you start to scale and grow your business, you naturally have learning curves when you don't know what you are doing. This is where beginner business mistakes can be inevitable. But you can learn so much from them, like I did in this situation.Business doesn't get easier. You just get smarter.

As I mentioned, the first year in my first studio was great. There were no problems whatsoever. So when the red flags started happening, I was taken aback and confused as to what I'd done to deserve this terrible sort of treatment. Not only did the landlord refuse to sit down and have a conversation with me in person, but he also wouldn't talk over the phone. That's when I knew something was off.

You would think that me deciding to leave the space—which I felt like he was trying to make me do anyway—would make him happy. He had a brand-new finished space that he could now rent out to multiple people because I had put up walls and divided it—and I'd paid for it. But no, my landlord was not satisfied with me choosing to simply leave. He was angry and out for some sort of strange vengeance that I don't think I'll ever understand completely. And I've had to just chalk that up to being part of my learning journey.

He made my life a living hell every day with his email notices about something else I had done wrong. While writing this, I went back to my emails to see what all he nagged me about, and I felt my heart beating faster as I read emails from this awful experience I wish I never had.

Have you ever had an experience like that? Where you can actually feel your body negatively responding when you think back or go back to photos, emails, or memories of the past? This is entrepreneurial trauma, and it's real. Just like any other trauma we live through, there are beginner business mistakes we all make that force us to learn lessons the hard way. While they are painful, they leave a mark on us—and we never make that mistake again!

My thirtysomething-year-old self, who's reading these emails, just wants to hug the young Stephanie, who thought she could just people-please her way out of some ugly experiences. My responses to the landlord's cold, demeaning, finger-pointing emails were kind and overaccommodating. We will sometimes never know why someone treats us the way they do, though, and I wish I had stood up for myself long before I felt I needed to.

Growth Lessons

As you start to scale and grow your business, you naturally have learning curves where you don't know what you are doing. This is where making beginner business mistakes can often be inevitable. But you can learn so much from them, like I did in this situation. As I said earlier, business doesn't get easier. You just get smarter. You will learn at some point, just like I did, that you have to protect your peace and your business because not everyone has good intentions. And you can't do business on a handshake.

Grace, Growth, and Gratitude

It was February 14, 2019, and I had just packed up the last remnants of my studio space. When I got home, I received an email from my attorney. My heart sank. I can still viscerally feel the pit in my stomach as I read the words my attorney had written: *He is going to pursue you for money.*

Why? How? I wondered. *What is going to happen?* And what did I do to deserve this? My mind was racing as my heart was beating out of my chest. I'm sure you know the feeling when you think back to your own entrepreneurial trauma.

I thought that when I left the space, all of my troubles with my now ex-landlord would just magically go away. But, in fact, quite the opposite happened. They got worse. But now, I was no longer receiving emails from him. They came via my attorney and his attorney, which only meant more and more money being added to my bill for every minute my attorney spent responding.

This initial email spiraled into an entire year of harassment by this man, who somehow thought he was going to get rich off a young, broke, twentysomething-year-old business owner. Not only did he take me to small claims court over thirty dollars instead of just asking for it via an invoice, but he then continued to sue me for what he deemed $25,000 worth of "damages" and "back rent" because we had verbally agreed I didn't owe rent until my space was finished and open for business.

I spent the majority of 2019 working my butt off just trying to make ends meet in my new studio space and dreading the day I would finally have to go to mediation and sit at a table with this person who'd grown to dislike me so strongly.

Following my attorney's advice, I gathered lots of photos of the space from before, during, and after my time there that showed how much I had not damaged, but rather improved, it for myself and the next tenant. I felt confident in my case, and I was ready to fight for it and finally stand up for myself!

My dad accompanied me to mediation since he was there the day I negotiated the lease. My attorney was there too, of course. And I even had my builder ready to make a statement for me if needed. But as soon as we sat down, unfortunately, it was clear that, unlike me, the judge was not willing to sit there all day. He started the mediation with "Okay. So how about we just meet in the middle and save us some time instead of going to arbitration?"

I turned to my attorney and asked, "What does he mean? Meet in the middle?"

My head was already calculating what "meet in the middle of $25,000" would mean, and I started to feel sick to my stomach . . . This was *not* how I saw this going.

My attorney spoke up, saying, "I'd like to meet with my client privately."

Thank God, I thought because I needed to understand what was happening.

So my dad, attorney, and I were escorted into a separate room, and my attorney explained it to me. He said, "The judge has already made up his mind. This is not going to end well for you if we go into arbitration."

I had learned the difference between meditation and arbitration. In mediation, both parties come to an agreement, which felt impossible considering the unreasonable mind of this man I was in conflict with. In arbitration, the judge would decide the verdict based on how the law would interpret the situation—which was not looking good for me.

Finally, the judge came in to bring insight, and it was exactly what I didn't want to hear. He said that, even though this man had harassed me for over a year and we'd had a verbal conversation about rent due, it wasn't in writing. Therefore, I would end up owing him something in back rent. If we went into arbitration, it would end up being more than necessary. So his solution was for me to pay my old landlord $5,000, he would keep my $1,000 security deposit, and we would call it a day. I swore he pulled that number out of thin air, but all I could think of was how I was going to come up with $5,000 for this to all go away.

I quickly accepted that this would be my fate and simply asked the judge, "Okay, $5,000. What does that look like? Because I don't have that much. But I could come up with monthly payments."

And, in words I will never forget because they made me feel like the smallest version of myself, he pointed at my dad and said, "Your dad's going to pay it, and you're going to pay him back."

I was the girl who'd gotten a job at fourteen because she didn't want to ask her parents for money and was determined to buy her own car. The girl who'd moved out into her own apartment at eighteen and paid for it all by herself. The girl who'd paid her way through college.

She now needed her dad to bail her out.

Enraged for obviously good reason, my dad responded, "What? How does that make any sense?"

And the judge replied, "Well, you loaned her thousands of dollars. What's another $5,000?"

This judge thought that my dad had loaned me all the money for my business and that I was some spoiled daddy's girl who wanted to make a go of opening my own yoga and fitness studio.

Never had I felt so misunderstood. So judged. And so disrespected.

I wondered what would have happened if I hadn't been a woman in a room surrounded by men. I wondered what would have happened if my dad hadn't been there with me that day. Would my fate have been better or worse? I'm not sure.

I walked out of that office with an experience that had taken away forever my naivety in life and in business.

Thankfully, my parents were willing and able to loan me the $5,000. My dad hugged me and told me not to pay him back because he knew I was already struggling to make ends meet.

But never again would I allow myself to go through such an experience all because I didn't properly read or understand my lease. That is why I'm so passionate about helping business owners make smart decisions when it comes to negotiating leases, running brick-and-mortar businesses, and protecting themselves legally. Because I did business on a handshake and assumed no one would ever try to take advantage of me.

Never again would I let a grown man harass me into thinking I didn't know anything. And never again would I think that I could just try to people-please myself out of a situation that was never in my best interests in the first place.

I realized through this chapter of my entrepreneurship journey that not everyone has your best interests at heart, you cannot do business on a handshake, and some people will take advantage of your age, gender, and lack of experience.

And despite how awful it was, I am extremely grateful for it.

It made me smarter, wiser, and a better businesswoman. It also made me appreciate what I would grow to have in my new space.

We may not always see it in the moment, but I have always tried to find the silver lining in a horrible experience. If it hadn't been for that crazy landlord pushing me out the door, I never would have had my second space or found what would turn out to be amazing landlords and a true mentor.

It is strange how, to this day, I don't feel any animosity toward my old landlord. I have only gratitude for what that experience led me to and how much it challenged me to grow.

It gave me an experience I wouldn't wish upon anybody. But it's also a story I can share with so many small business owners about how to avoid these situations themselves. The whole time I was going through that dark experience, I just kept telling myself, *If I can help at least one person avoid this situation or, if they are in the thick of it, come out on the other side better instead of bitter, it will be worth it.*

So, while I can joke about it now with past members and staff who were with me during that strange experience, it left a mark on my heart. I knew it was a turning point in my journey that completely changed my path for the better. But I didn't know it when I was going through it. I was just trying to keep my head above water.

Yet these are the stories of entrepreneurial trauma that keep me humble and relatable, no matter what amount of business success I have achieved. While I am far past this chapter in my journey, I can still feel the pain. Just going back through those emails to write this chapter has me feeling all the emotions of that season again.

I don't candidly share this chapter often or in detail because, like I said, I've moved on. And although I have so much gratitude, it is still very painful.

I'll never forget this experience of growth, overcoming, and taking the high road to be the bigger person. So many people told me to sue him back or bash his business. But I didn't. I wished him well, moved on, and honestly shoved all the emotions away in a drawer I never looked in—until writing this.

You realize you're on the other side of dark seasons when you notice glimmers of growth and healing all around you, especially in the little things.

I recently met with an attorney because I've learned through hard lessons, like this chapter, to be proactive and no longer reactive in my business. Plus, I'm always looking to build my network of business resources. I didn't realize until I got to the attorney's office that it was the same place where I met my ex-landlord for mediation—the one who filed that lawsuit against me what feels like many moons ago.

All I could do was smile and laugh to myself when I walked by the conference room. That meeting was one of the worst days of my life as an entrepreneur, and it taught me many lessons I'll never forget. It was such a moment of grace, growth, and gratitude for the hard seasons I had to walk through as a young twenty-year-old. Walking by that room made me realize how far I've come and all I've learned from that traumatic experience.

Find gratitude for the hard seasons you overcame that made you who you are just as much as all the good God has brought you. Keep looking for your own glimmers of healing and growth—they will give you life to keep going.

This was not my first experience of holding my head high and moving forward with grit and grace. But little did I know how much this mindset would serve me in hard seasons and how this awful experience would catapult me into finding the mentor I needed.

Growth Lessons

Find grace to hold your head high and take the high road when you've been wronged. Use your growth and see the purpose in your pain: to help others avoid the mistakes you've made. Trust me. When it is traumatic, painful, and awful to go through, you'll never forget it or make the same mistake again! Find gratitude for lessons learned the hard way, as they make you who you are and allow you to appreciate all the ups and downs along your entrepreneurial journey. If you're new at business, just know you'll have your own growing pains. We all do. So try to embrace them. If you've been at it a while, you know exactly what I'm talking about, and I commend you for getting through those hard seasons. Continue to find grace and gratitude because they are some of your biggest growth seasons.

When the Student Is Ready, the Mentor Appears

I am a firm believer that when the student is ready, the mentor appears. I still find it hard to believe that I spent my first six years of small business ownership basically winging it. Yet when I got the red flags from my landlord telling me I needed to leave my studio space, I knew that the main reason I jumped into a brand-new space with high overhead was that I was hoping to gain a mentor. I was desperate to learn from someone who could steer me in the right direction and would be willing to be transparent about the seasons of small business ownership. And Misty was just that.

When I took a bet on myself to make a big, scary decision to up-level my business and move my studio from Holmen to Onalaska, Wisconsin, I knew it was a huge risk. While I felt like I didn't have a choice in whether I wanted to move or not (thanks to my ex-landlord), I did have a choice in where I decided to go. I chose to take a big financial risk to invest in a build-out in Misty's Dance Unlimited because I knew I could possibly gain an amazing mentor.

What I didn't realize, though, was that I would not only gain a mentor but be pulled into an entire community of growth-minded, encouraging dance studio owners from across the globe. Misty had grown and cultivated a community of high-level dance studio owners in her company, More Than Just Great Dancing, who gathered to learn and grow online together each month. Then, twice a year, they came together in person at their live events, Studio Owner University (SOU) and Member Rally.

In the cold winter, before my build-out was even complete, she texted me, Hey I would love for you to join us at SOU Palm Springs in February, free ticket on me!

Well, she didn't have to ask me twice to leave the Wisconsin winter *and* that year's polar vortex to get me to travel to Palm Springs. It meant a lot to me that she even invited me, so I booked myself a flight. Her team helped me find a fellow member as a roommate, and I had no idea what I was in for.

I was blown away by the kindness and warm-hearted welcomes from her group. I didn't know a single soul there but immediately felt like I was part of the pack. I spent three days listening to speakers share their inspiring stories of overcoming challenges within their studios. For the first time, I'd found a community of business owners who believed in doing business and life well. They had grown teams, owned multiple studios, and enjoyed more financial and time freedom than I could ever imagine.

Needless to say, I was inspired.

At this time, I was taking on more debt than I could grasp in order to overcome the hardships from my previous space and that nasty lawsuit. I knew the year ahead would pose more challenges for me in growing my own team, increasing my sales, and, ultimately, beginning to dig my way out of the hole I had sunk into. So, a community to push me, inspire me, and encourage me was exactly what I needed.

I walked in feeling like I didn't belong in this room of business owners because:

1. I wasn't a dancer or dance studio owner.
2. They were light-years ahead of me in every area, not to mention I was probably the youngest in the room.
3. I didn't know a soul.

Here's what I came to learn after that first Studio Owner University: Anytime Misty invites me to do something, I say *yes!* That "one small yes," as she says in her book, was another true turning point in my life. I learned so much at my first SOU in Palm Springs.

It was the first real business conference I had ever been to, and we dug into our numbers, our marketing plans, how to create systems, and, ultimately, how to lead a team well. Those were all of my areas of interest as a business owner. But prior to meeting my mentor, I wouldn't have had the opportunity right in front of me to learn about them from someone I knew who had successfully done them in her own business. A mentor who practices what they preach and teaches from a place of experience is everything. There are many business coaches out there today who are teaching and preaching without the experience to back it up. Not only did Misty have years of experience as a seasoned soul-preneur, but she extended to her own experienced studio owners the opportunity to become coaches and speakers too.

When I saw all the certified coaches on stage, I thought, I hope that's me up there someday, sharing my own story and experience of overcoming. If I implement everything I learn from this community, I can share my own journey to help inspire others to keep going too.

Having Misty as a mentor gave me the opportunity to attend my first SOU. But I was able to continue my learning and integrating every month on the business calls I was invited to show up to. So I went all in. Not only did I show up for every single monthly coaching call, but I also implemented and integrated everything I was learning. And that's the real key right there! If you're not going to put in the effort to implement what you're learning, you're missing the point.

If you're looking to find the right mentor for your small business journey, there are lots of ways to do so. If you're just getting started or are building your business on a budget, you might start with someone you don't know but could learn from, like a podcast host, author, speaker, or someone you follow on Instagram. While this isn't a personal relationship, it allows you to try and find the right person for you without a more formal commitment. Make sure you vet that they know what they are talking about and have years of experience to back it up. Who knows—maybe you'll even meet them someday to make them more than just someone you follow online.

If you are looking for more formal mentorship, it might look more like business coaching. Of course, you can pay to be part of a coaching cohort or even a community like the one I was part of. This steps up your level of commitment to learning *and* integrating because you're paying for it. This can be very helpful in certain seasons when you need that extra accountability and personal mentorship. Again, make sure to vet the coach or program you are paying for and make sure they are legitimate and the right fit for you, your business, and your personal and professional goals. Make sure the lifestyle they are living is desirable to you so that you are aligned with your values.

Lastly, I firmly believe that when you ask, the Universe delivers just the right person, so don't be afraid to put it out there that you're searching for a personal mentor. This is more informal and not paid. But it gives you a guide on your journey at just the right time to offer wisdom and encouragement when you need them most. This is what my mentor has been to me—a guiding light when I needed it most. I was fortunate that our paths crossed when they did. That's why I believe you can also find your version of this when you are open to receiving it. Or, if you have someone in mind, find the courage to straight up ask them to mentor you. The worst thing they can say is no. That means it isn't a good fit for you anyway. You'll just continue to search for the right person who says an enthusiastic *yes*!

Growth Lessons

Find a mentor who has done what you're trying to do or something similar, knows the way, and is willing to show you the way. Not only is learning from a mentor important, but implementing what you learn is the key to success. You can read books, listen to podcasts, go to business conferences, and take in an overwhelming amount of education, but it doesn't matter unless you apply it and figure out if it works for you. It's such a privilege to learn firsthand from someone you trust, like a mentor. But if you learn without integrating, you're wasting time and energy. You're also telling your mentor that you don't value the valuable time they're spending to teach you.

Show them you are worth the investment and ask for their advice without taking advantage of their time, then tell and show them how what they've shared with you has helped you reach your goals. There's nothing better than getting a text from people I've mentored, telling me how they've implemented my advice and how it helped them for the better!

Chapter Reflections

Reflection Questions:

❖ Have you made any of the beginner business mistakes mentioned in this chapter? How did it make you a better business owner?

❖ Is there a mistake you've made that you continue to beat yourself up for? Why?

❖ How can you reframe your story about a mistake you made? Or how you trusted someone who disappointed you, then gave yourself grace and gratitude for the growth?

❖ What values, advice, and strategy do you look for in a mentor?

❖ Where have you integrated what you've learned from a mentor? How has it positively affected you and your business?

Intentional Action:

• New Small Business Owner: We all make beginner mistakes, so continue to give yourself grace by finding gratitude for the growth lessons you've learned along the way. I encourage you to find a mentor sooner rather than later to help you lessen the pain in some of the beginner's mistakes—or maybe even avoid some altogether—and ultimately even out the highs and lows of the entrepreneurial roller coaster. Find a mentor who fits with your values and the lifestyle and business you want to build. They could possibly even be specific to your industry. Ask them to mentor you—and make sure to thank them for their insight and advice, then do the work!

- Seasoned Small Business Owner: At this point in the game, my guess is you have a mentor. If not, take the advice I gave the new small business owner and get yourself a guide! If you do have a mentor, or even a few mentors, by this point, *thank* them. This could be giving them a handwritten note with a gift card to their favorite coffee shop (my personal love language), mailing a personal gift you know they will love, or simply leaving a voice memo letting them know how much they have positively impacted your life. Be sure to share with them how the guidance or advice they've given has worked, then ask how you can *help them*. While they may not give you a tangible way to help them, be sure to let them know you are there to support them and their goals too.

Lease signing day for my third studio with my mentor, Misty Lown
(2019)

Chapter 6:

Hustle with Heart

Getting Gritty with Your Resources

The day I signed the lease, I took photos to make the big announcement that my new studio was coming soon. I signed the lease, and Misty asked me to meet at her office and show her my floor plan. I was thrilled to be part of this brand-new building and create my business dreams alongside her twenty-plus-year vision. She was all in on adding a fitness and yoga studio to her building and was very encouraging to me about continuing with my plans.

I wanted the space to feel light and bright, so I picked out all the paint colors. Of course I picked a bright teal for an accent wall in the gym to glow in the sunshine that poured in from all the windows, as well as a soft teal and gray in the yoga room that would provide the Zen experience I was going for. The flooring was a beautiful gray wood in all rooms except the gym. This was my dream studio, so I was finally ordering an expensive black rubber flooring for the gym—something I had wished for from the beginning of my business. I ultimately designed the entire space myself. Heck, I even painted a few of the rooms. To say I put my blood, sweat, tears, and every penny I didn't even have yet into this studio space is an understatement.

While I signed the lease in December, we had to get the state's approval of the architectural floor plans, which didn't come back until the middle of January. Meaning we couldn't start construction until after the plans were approved. It was stressful because this space needed everything—electric, drywall, heating and air conditioning, flooring, bathrooms, painting, you name it. And the lease I was leaving was up in February.

Of course, because we were in Wisconsin, we were experiencing the polar vortex that winter. If you're unfamiliar with this phenomenon, it basically means it's colder than a normal winter—yikes! Therefore, lots of items I had chosen, like doors and windows, were delayed. We were shooting for a soft opening in March. We were going to open to just our members for a week and have our grand opening on the Saturday following. *There is no way we are going to get this all done in time*, I thought. So I had to get creative.

When my lease ended in February, I was studio-less for a few weeks. So I got gritty with my resources and planned pop-ups all over town. We did a chakra yoga balancing workshop at a local salon that had Ayurveda oils. We did our famous barre at the bar at the local distillery. We did a meditation workshop at a local boutique. The dance studio was even kind enough to let us use their studio rooms when they were vacant to hold a few classes. It was a super-fun time, popping all over, marketing our new studio, and building all the hype as I used social media to take people behind the scenes into the process of the build-out.

The week we were hoping to soft open was fast approaching, and I knew we weren't going to be able to finish. So I jumped on Facebook Live that week for a few fun live-streamed workouts. (Yes,

I was doing pop-ups and even live-streaming workouts *way* before it was a thing.)

To say that week was stressful is an understatement. We needed all hands on board to help get the studio ready for the grand opening, and my main contractor came down with the flu. My new landlord's husband jumped in to save the day and did all the bathroom tile. My dad's friend Randy came and helped install all the doors. Our instructors' husbands were helping us move equipment and do floors and trim. It was *insanity.*

Finally, the Friday before our Saturday grand opening, we needed the city inspector to approve everything, or we weren't going to be able to open. I was so nervous for him to come walking through and give the final approval. The trim on the doors, windows, and floors still wasn't done, but we were hoping it was good enough for his approval so we could open.

The inspector showed up later in the afternoon, walked through quickly, and said, "Yep, you're good to go."

I was shocked. It was that fast and easy? Well," I said. "I guess tomorrow we are opening!"

While ideally, I was hoping to have a few classes that week to work out kinks before our grand opening, I've learned in entrepreneurship that you often just have to roll with the punches. For our grand opening, we offered a few different free mini classes, prizes, and a promotion on memberships.

The studio was *packed.* It was exactly what I had envisioned. Lots of our current members and lots of new faces were signing up too. Everyone was so excited and in awe of the beautiful brand-new studio. I was so proud of what we had accomplished in just two months by rallying a great team of contractors and, of course, my own team, who helped me tremendously in bringing this vision to life.

After the grand opening, I knew the real work would begin. I knew I had just signed up for four times the expenses of my previous studio, which meant my sales needed to also quadruple just to break even.

I thought, Here we go . . .

Having the right resources in your life and business and being creative can make or break you in times of challenge—like when I opened my new studio space on a time crunch. Resources don't always mean money either. Resources like education, community, ideas, support, or people to help you on your journey can often be even more valuable than just the financial means to build your dream.

2019 became the definition of a hustle year for me when it came to getting gritty and getting to work. I was averaging teaching twenty to thirty classes per week and running on adrenaline and caffeine–which seemed to be a common theme in my twenties.

I had the business loan, but now I needed to pay it off. And that took building up my book of resources.

As I mentioned, I dove headfirst into learning business strategy, developing ideas, and gaining support from my mentor and her community of dance studio owners. I showed up on every weekly call and implemented what I learned with my team. Then it was on to the next thing. The pace we were scaling at was fast because we didn't have time to sit in the negative. We needed to get to the green and get profitable ASAP!

Marketing was so important for getting the word out about our new space. So I continued to build my network and get in front of more people through free pop-up events in the studio and out and about in our community. We built great partnerships with many local small businesses that we would collaborate with and cross-promote to our audiences. And when I say I got gritty, I mean I was doing boots-on-the-ground marketing, knocking on doors of local small businesses to get in front of their employees, clients, and anyone who would be willing to come try a free class with us.

I was also extremely focused on building a strong system for marketing, which included using our social media platforms, like Facebook and Instagram; keeping our website and Google page up to date; and performing email marketing. Each week, I followed a consistent strategy of showing up on social media so we never skipped a beat. I had my interns help create content as long as I came up with the overarching theme of the posts each week.

I was still the visionary driver of our marketing. But with systems in place, I could have my team help me create the actual content and post it for engagement. Was it always how I would have created it? No. But I came to learn that done is usually better than perfect. Also, I often created templates in Canva and our email software so that each marketing message was cohesive and represented our brand how I envisioned it.

As I started to grow my team behind the front desk to do more admin work, the need for systems and structure became even more apparent. This is where I learned from my mentor's community about a rhythms calendar and task management programs. I took intentional time out of my business to do a brain dump for every task in the business that is repeated on a daily, weekly, monthly, quarterly, and annual rhythm. Then I categorized tasks—like finances, marketing, sales, team, clients, etc.—and organized it all into a task management program called Asana.

The beauty of a task management program is that you can set it to recur. That way, if it's weekly, it shows up on your task to-do list every single week. If it's monthly, it shows up every month, and so on. You can also assign tasks to your staff and track what they have completed each week so you don't need to micromanage their productivity. You do the same for project-based tasks that are not recurring. Integrating a rhythmic calendar and Asana allowed me to break down huge projects, keep track of the millions of tasks I do as a small business owner, and offload some of the responsibility onto my growing team.

I also became very intentional about something so many small business owners shy away from—*selling*! I learned how to sell and built up an entire sales system (which went into our task management system, of course) for attracting new leads through our marketing system. I also learned how to get those leads into our internal sales funnel to continue on as members. We invited leads to join us for their first class free and encouraged them to do a thirty-day challenge trial or a class pack. Then we worked on getting them to commit to becoming a member. We got extremely focused on not just converting new leads into members but retaining members through exclusive client events, rewards, discounts, special acknowledgments of birthdays and milestones, and so much more. This focus on sales was inspired by my mentor and what her community taught me about implementing a salesforce.

So many small businesses want to be in business but hate selling. Sales is the lifeblood of the business. You can't make a positive impact in the world by selling your product or service without money coming in from sales. In fact, you don't have a business without selling. So why not get intentional about how you want to attract, convert, and onboard new clients into your business so you can continue to sell to them or get referrals from your loyal clients? Trust me, business is more fun when you have sales rolling in! Not to mention, nobody sells your business better than *you*. So, as the owner, learn to fall in love with selling.

When it came to getting resourceful, I knew I needed to build a team of people to help grow the business. So I reached out to the local universities to build a partnership for internships. We had many fantastic interns who brought us great ideas and fresh energy. And, of course, they were young and tech-savvy when it came to social media!

Some were exercise sports science interns who got to gain hands-on experience working with clients; others were business and marketing interns who worked our front desk, greeted clients, handled marketing, and promoted events and classes. Interns who provided time and energy in exchange for my mentorship on business, fitness, and yoga were a valuable resource that brought so much joy to me and to them. In fact, many stayed on as employees after their internships.

I also continued to grow our team of instructors so we could offer more classes and services, and I started building out my own framework for leading teacher training opportunities. I learned the value of building systems for everything in a business and knew I needed to streamline training so we could continue to grow faster and have our instructors all be on the same page in our teaching methodology.

But in all of the ten years I had the studio, I found the most success in training up clients to become instructors. They were so much more committed to the business, vision, and values than people I hired from outside our community who simply submitted their resumes and didn't understand what we were all about.

With more staff, we were able to ramp up our classes, offering them throughout the entire day to maximize our studio space—including holding two classes at once during the popular times of five a.m. and five p.m. Things were really taking off! As you can imagine, doing all of this at once meant I was working pretty much twenty-four-seven and was on a fast track to burnout. While I hustled so hard, I'm grateful I found the right person to help me balance my hustle with heart.

Growth Lessons

Search out the right resources for your own success. Also, know that you can solve any problem when you get gritty with your strategy and the support you build around your business. As I started to scale to include a team of instructors and interns, I learned very quickly that I needed to implement systems, fast. There's no point in bringing people in to help you grow your business when you don't have the systems in place to train them and give them clear values, a mission, and a vision to work toward.

Maybe you want to grow, but you forget about the challenges that come along with scaling. That's why scaling sustainably with systems for sales, marketing, and training is so essential. Remember when I said business doesn't get easier? You just get smarter and wiser? This chapter of expanding my business is a perfect example of that. You get smarter when you look within your obstacles for opportunities to get resourceful and creative. Always be on the lookout to build your resources along your small business journey. And remember that resources are so much more than just money!

From Training Partner to Life Partner

Remember when I told you I started training MMA to move on from all the crappy, awful boyfriend situations I had in college? Yeah, well, you know what they say—the moment you stop focusing on finding the right person, that's the second they find you. I was not interested in taking my focus off my business or MMA training, which I guess is why God decided to bring my person right to me.

We have to go back a little bit on my journey to the summer of 2014 . . .

I still recall the day that Ben Ross walked into Iron Works gym. It was the middle of our fight camp as I was preparing for my first fight. He walked in wearing a black tank top. And I cannot tell you why, but I just distinctly remember thinking, *That's him! I'm going to marry him.* He still laughs at me and doesn't believe me to this day, but my intuition has always been strong, and I just had an odd gut feeling that he was the person who would complete my hustle + heart equation.

But don't let me fool you. It was *not* all romantic. In fact, I'm pretty sure he puked his guts out that day because he came on the worst day. Our coach was making us run sprints *forever* until everyone finished. It was a brutal practice. I thought, *Yikes, I wonder if he and his roommate will even come back.*

Well, there they were the next day and the day after that. I soon learned they were going to school at Winona State and driving to the gym, about a thirty-minute drive each way, every day, just to train MMA.

He was, let's just say, interesting and mysterious. He didn't say much, but he was very handsome. He was tall, had short dark hair, and had some build to him. What intrigued me most was the intensity about him. I wouldn't say he was unfriendly, but he wasn't warm and bubbly like me. And he didn't seem very interested in chatting or getting to know anyone. It was clear that he was there to train and that was his focus.

Aside from the first day, one day in particular stands out to me. A few days after we met, he showed up for wrestling practice. Well, I was the only girl there that day, and no one was near my size. In all honesty, I probably shouldn't have joined in practice. That's the hard thing about being a girl in MMA: We hardly ever had any girl training partners, and even the guys were a lot bigger and stronger.

Well, Ben became my partner. We were playing king of the mat, where one person is in the middle and the other has to out-wrestle them to become the king. Ben was in the middle, and even though wrestling was not his strong point at the time, he easily had size and strength on me! He had a grip on my neck and then snapped it down, resulting in me having a pinched nerve in my neck. There were tears. The coach called me out and told me to sit out the rest of the game because I couldn't compete with them anyway. I guess my "I'll prove I'm tough" attitude didn't work out for me that day.

The goal was not to injure our teammates in practice. But, obviously, when you're that much bigger and stronger, it's hard to know your own strength. And I was mad about it. The next day, Ben tried to come up to me before practice and apologize for hurting my neck and making me cry. I replied, "Whatever," as I got up and walked away.

From then on, it was obvious he did not want to train with me for fear of injuring me and, I'm sure, the attitude he'd have to deal with after the fact. But the coaches kept saying, "Ben, you have to hit her. She has a fight coming up!" I can't imagine how awkward that was for him and most of the guys I was training with.

Well, we got to know each other a little bit over the course of that fight camp. Ben fought right after my humiliating loss and won!

I was right back at the gym after my loss, feeling fired up and wanting to continue training. He was also back at the gym after his win, and we connected more in practice since a lot of our teammates took time off after their fights. But we didn't.

Finally, after practice one day, he invited me to come up to Winona and go out with him and his friends for homecoming that weekend. I tried to find a friend to go with me. I figured that would be much better if it turned out awkward. Of course, everyone was busy. But something in my gut told me to just go. I've learned to listen to that little voice inside me, so I drove to Winona all by myself.

Even though I knew only Ben and his roommate, we went out and had the best time. People kept mistaking us for a couple the entire night . . . which I guess said something, as we'd just look at each other and smile.

I stayed in Winona because I obviously wasn't going to make a forty-minute drive home after bar time. I thought, *Gosh, this is going to be so awkward in the morning.* I mean, you have to remember that not only were we teammates, but my business was at the gym. That could have ruined a lot of things. But I awoke in the morning to

Ben making me breakfast, and we laughed and reminisced about the night over coffee. I guess you could say that after that night, the rest is history.

Ben and I started dating two weeks later. We had a few bumps right in the beginning as we figured each other out and saw how we were so different in a lot of ways. But MMA and working out were our commonalities, so we bonded over that in the beginning.

After Ben's roommates all graduated and left Winona, he moved in with me in La Crosse after only six months of dating, and we've lived together ever since. We've been together now for over a decade.

Ben started as my training partner, turned into my boyfriend, and became my best friend in life. When I decided I wanted to train to fight again, he was my biggest supporter and helped me become better so I could get in the cage and finally get a *win*!

I share this story of meeting Ben because I believe we meet the right people for us in unexpected places when we are not focusing on what we lack. And that's true of business as well as life. Embrace the unexpected surprises and don't forget to have things and people in your life that remind you to enjoy life while growing your business.

I didn't know when I met Ben that he was the sounding board and support I needed for the highs and lows of my small business journey. Even though I'm sure there were plenty of times he didn't know what to say or how to help, his consistent presence in my life and ability to listen were often all I needed.

From being there through the lawsuit with my ex-landlord to supporting me as I scaled my studio—often at the cost of my personal life—Ben was just that for me. There were many years when he was able to support us financially as I struggled to get the business into profitability. There were also many nights when I came home at nine p.m. to find him waiting for me with dinner on the table. He was there with me from my humble beginnings and through my studio successes and my very low lows. And he always continued to surprise me.

Growth Lessons

You have to find the people who help you balance hustle with heart and support you from the very start, whether that's a significant other, friend, or family member. We all need people who remind us who we are and who we can have fun with on our entrepreneurial journey.

I firmly believe that some people are just meant to cross your path at the right time. Trusting my gut to get to know Ben and take a chance on him is a perfect example of that. When you follow your intuition and trust your journey, the right people will present themselves. I'll touch on it more later, but you also learn in business that some people are with you for a season while others join you for the entire journey. Having people who come along on your business journey, support you from the beginning, and go through every evolution is one of the biggest gifts you could ever ask for. I had the hustle from the very beginning, but adding the heart to the equation was a bonus!

Hustling with Heart

It was Saturday, April 22, 2019. And more importantly, it was fight night for our local fight card. While I had given up competing in MMA when I left Iron Works, Ben had continued to train and fight since. He had been training hard for this fight night, as he always does, while I was working sixteen-hour days, hyper-focused on building my dream studio. But I had yet to miss a fight night. So, after spending Saturday at the studio, I ran home for a quick break before heading to cheer Ben on in his big fight.

I specifically remember Ben asking me before I left the apartment that day, "Is that what you're wearing tonight?"

I gave him a look, "My lululemon leggings and Zen and Pow cropped sweatshirt with sneakers isn't good enough?" I said teasingly. "Yes, this is comfortable, so this is what I'm wearing."

"Okay."

And that was all he said. I thought it was strange because he never commented on my clothing.

He was one of the later fights. So, when I got to the arena, I finally let loose a bit from all the work I'd been doing. I always get nervous when I watch him fight, so I had a few drinks. His opponent came in way overweight, but Ben still agreed to fight him. Only 2:15 into Round 1, Ben landed a hard punch and won by TKO—knockout! The announcer began to interview him, which is normal.

But at the very end, the announcer said, "Ben, you have made your mark here in the Midwest as a professional MMA fighter. Is there anything else you want to say? The stage is yours." And he handed the mic to Ben.

Ben responded, "Yeah, one other thing . . . Stephanie Helmers, could you please come up to the cage? I got something I want to ask you."

I was in shock and could not stop smiling as I made my way into the cage.

The promoter and gym owner, whom I'd known since I started at Iron Works, handed Ben a ring box through the cage. The crowd began to cheer loudly as Taylor Swift's "Our Song" began to play. It was simply perfect.

As I walked into the cage, Ben was red and sweaty from his fight. He put his mouth guard behind his ear and opened the box with his fight gloves still on. Then he kneeled to ask me his question: "Will you marry me?"

At this point, I was crying *and* laughing. I don't think I even answered his question. He picked me up, and I wrapped my legs around him. I just wanted to stay there in that moment forever. Ben then set me down to try and put the ring on my finger.

Laughing, I said, "I don't even know which finger it goes on!" Because this is how much I didn't know about rings, jewelry, engagements—any of it. I was just so surprised and in the moment.

We finally made our way out of the cage, and Ben looked relieved. I can't imagine the amount of stress and pressure he'd been under from not only trying to win his fight but then propose in front of a couple thousand people while wanting it to all go perfectly. Which it did.

That may have been the one thing in 2019 that surprised me the most—in the *best* way—and felt magically perfect. I was on a high for the rest of the weekend. Ben had done a fantastic job picking out my ring, considering I had never given him the slightest idea about my taste in rings and we'd never even looked at any. I couldn't stop looking at it.

Then Monday set in, and it was back to the hustle. But I had a new motivation to try and save for a wedding! But in all honesty, I knew having this dream space required rolling up my sleeves even more. And I'd never been afraid of hard work. I was always up for a challenge, and I met it. With all I had learned from Misty and her company, More Than Just Great Dancing, I had implemented so much that we'd almost doubled our original membership number of fifty when we started in March to nearly a hundred by the end of the year.

As the summer passed and it faded to fall, Ben and I picked a wedding date and our venue—a barn wedding on our anniversary, November 7, 2020. Our engagement photos were in October, and it snowed! I found my dress, and the wedding planning began. Despite the amount of work I had and the stress I was under, I was enjoying picking out all the colors and details of our big day. It was the perfect distraction from the overwhelming amount of work (not to mention the lawsuit I was going through that year).

I started to get a strange nudge to create an online platform for Zen and Pow toward the end of that year. I can't explain why, but it was an idea I wanted to explore. I put out an ad for an intern who could help me, and along came Tara. She took my ideas and built them into an online website specifically for on-demand classes that members could access at any time for prerecorded workouts with us. I wasn't exactly sure what I was going to do with this website, but it was just another nudge I followed into the new year.

2019 finally came to a close. And considering all I had been through, man, was I glad to close the door on that year. It was a big year of growth, expansion, and implementation, but I was proud of how far I had come. I was also looking forward to reaching our membership goals in 2020.

While I was teetering on the edge of burnout after that insane year, I could finally see the light at the end of the tunnel. 2020 was going to be *our year*. I had huge goals for the business *and* our wedding, and I finally felt like I had some stability, considering I had just been through the hardest year of my life.

Or so I thought . . .

I was so grateful to have the distraction of wedding planning with Ben because it felt like everything else in my business was swirling around me, from scaling to overcoming the lawsuit. I needed healthy distractions. Thankfully, my fiancé, friends, and family helped me find ways to take my mind off whatever challenges I was facing in my business while also supporting me along the journey.

In February 2020, we had reached our highest membership numbers to date—ninety-six members—which was just short of our goal of a hundred. We were just starting to consistently break even each month, and *green* was on the horizon for our profitability.

Growth Lessons

No matter what is happening in your business, it's so essential to find ways to have fun in your personal life so you don't burn out and make your life and identity all about your business. Thankfully, my engagement kept me busy with wedding planning. But, to be honest, I lost a lot of time for myself and my hobbies in that year of hustling. I don't recommend that. I learned the hard way how easy it is to lose yourself in your business when you're trying to grow fast and need to get gritty to get to profitability.

Whether it's friends, family, or a significant other, have people and hobbies around you that can help you take your mind off your challenges while also supporting you in your mission. When your entire life becomes your business, it starts to take over your identity. And when that happens, you're high on life when you're up. But when you're down, you feel like a personal failure. Find ways to find balance in your life and business so you can weather any storm as a business owner with the equation of hustle + heart.

Ben proposing to me in the cage (2019)

Chapter Reflections

Reflection Questions:

- ❖ In what ways do you need to get grittier with your resources to grow your business—marketing, sales, systems, staff, etc.?
- ❖ Where do you need to build your systems to scale sustainably over time so you don't burn out?
- ❖ How much of your identity is tied to your business? Are the highs and lows attached to your self-worth?
- ❖ Who are the people—significant other, family members, or friends—who can pull you out of your business and help you focus on your personal life outside your business?
- ❖ What hobbies and activities do you enjoy outside work that fill up your cup?

Intentional Action:

- New Small Business Owner: I have lots of advice in this chapter for the new small business owner when it comes to getting gritty and building smart from the start with systems. Just start recording everything you do, even if it's just writing it down in a notebook or doing a brain dump into a Google doc, like I did with my rhythms calendar. Start with the activities you do every day, week, month, quarter, and year, then get them on a rhythm so you're not dropping balls. Record the process of tasks, beginning with what you would like to hire or delegate so you have direction to give someone when you assign a task. This is the most basic form of systems you should start with. Then let them evolve from there. Oh, and *learn to love sales*! Seriously, if you make selling fun and create a system that works, it will solve many of your problems from the beginning and help you create profitability from the start.

- Seasoned Small Business Owner: I hope you have systems and processes in place by now so you can outsource, delegate, and train up team members to help take some of the responsibility off your plate. If not, start with the advice above and get to delegating. You don't need a full-time staff member to take on tasks that you don't enjoy doing and are not the best use of your time. Start with part-time help, interns, or a virtual assistant. You can also outsource. You may not be hustling at this point in your business journey, so I hope you're focusing on more of the *heart* and enjoying the freedom that entrepreneurship brings. Remember, systems bring sustainability and, ultimately, *freedom*! Finally, if you haven't pulled your identity away from your business, now is a good time to work on finding out who you are outside of what you *do*. Pour back into yourself with hobbies and people who lift you up so you're not burned out and in a bad relationship with your business by the time you find your balance.

Small Business Sister Story: Michelle Malone

Turning Doubts into Dreams

I had always dreamed of being a backup dancer on tour, and I was fully prepared to move to Los Angeles at age twenty-five to pursue that dream. Then I got pregnant, and it was a turning-point moment.

My dream of moving to LA was now out of the picture; my boyfriend and I couldn't afford to move there, nor did I want to be that far away from family. The season of becoming a mom was difficult for me. I loved my independence and I didn't have it anymore . . . I had a little baby depending on me for his every need. My son's father also made extremely bad decisions, so he was not involved. It was just me raising my son, trying to pay all the bills and give us somewhat of a joyful life.

Fast-forward five years . . . I am working a nine-to-five sales and marketing job in a cubicle. My son is five years old and just starting kindergarten, and I find myself extremely unhappy, unfulfilled, and lonely. I was living in survival mode. I was unhappy in my career. I didn't have many good friendships. And the biggest thing: I wasn't dancing anymore! The responsibilities and anxieties of being a single mom overtook my life, but I knew that something needed to change. I didn't want this to be my life anymore. I wanted to be happy again, feel fulfilled and be doing what I loved: dancing!

When I look back, I know this was the moment that changed the trajectory of my future. It was the moment that I changed my *mindset*.

I decided, after five years of fighting it, that I had to accept the fact that I lived in the small town of La Crosse, WI, because I needed the help and support of my parents close by. I knew I also couldn't financially afford to travel as often as I would like to go take dance classes even in the Midwest, so I decided that I had to create that outlet for myself.

So I went for it. I sought out the advice of business mentors in my life at the time, including Stephanie Ross. I was able to secure a $10K grant to get started and signed a lease for a small studio space in downtown La Crosse. I did this so fast that I couldn't even dwell on all the doubts running through my mind!

"Is anyone going to sign up for classes?" "Will this work out?" "Will I have enough money to pay the bills?" "What am I doing?" were running through my mind. But instead of listening to the fear-driven thoughts, I consistently kept working to change my mindset and reframe them into "But what if it does take off?" "What if it *does* work out?" "If only one person's life is impacted by this studio, this is worth it."

I got to a point where the risk of trying was greater than looking back and regretting that I didn't go for this dream of mine. It was and still is a constant, daily shifting of my mindset to keep thinking positively, with growth in mind.

So on January 23, 2023, I opened my dance studio in La Crosse, WI, exclusively for adults, and it was the best yet scariest decision I have ever made!

I knew I had a lot to learn because I did not go to college for business, so I joined Stephanie's business group, Sister Circle, to surround myself with the training and support I needed to be successful in business. I know that I would not be where I am today without this group of female business owners and the mentorship that Stephanie has brought to me. And guess what we probably talk about more than anything: mindset.

The first year of business was so exciting, but also so exhausting. It was all hands on deck for me. I was teaching all the classes, doing all the marketing, building my systems, paying the bills, cleaning the studio, etc. Yet . . . it was the most rewarding thing I have ever pushed through.

Now two years into the studio, natural leaders began to rise and I was able to pass off half of my teaching schedule to other instructors who encapsulate my culture of safe, welcoming, and fun dance classes for adults. I met these dancers because I opened my studio! I never knew how many adult dancers lived in our small town . . . It astounded me!

My adult dance students have now become some of my closest friends, and I have created connections in the community that have opened so many doors for my business. *This* is what I was craving, and I never knew that my studio was going to fulfill that deep longing in my soul for true connection and community right where I lived. It was the definition of dreaming big in a small town and seeing those dreams come to life!

The impact that dance is having on the community here is incredible, and it's because I decided to change my *mindset* and go for it despite my fears and doubts. When I hear feedback such as "This studio has saved my love for dance" and "It brought me so much joy to dance again," I know that this decision to grow this business was 100% worth it.

Small Business Sister Story: Rebecca Mattie

From Hustle to Harmony: Rebuilding My Business for
Balance and Joy

I started my business, Honeybee OT, to dictate my own schedule and how I served my clients. I knew what a successful practice looked like, and I wanted to get there as soon as possible. I entered full-time entrepreneurship and opened my own brick-and-mortar clinic after about only eighteen months in practice because I saw the consistent growth already happening.

Then I had the opportunity to take a big leap into a larger space of my own. The possibilities for more growth in a new space were astronomical, and all I could see were the big dreams I had and the asset this could become for our community. Leading up to signing the lease, it felt like all the pieces were falling into place between family support, earning a grant, and generous landlords willing to negotiate my lease to grow with me. I dove headfirst into running my own brick-and-mortar pediatric therapy clinic.

After only a year in the new space though, I was already burning out. My schedule was maxed out beyond what it ever was when I was working for someone else. I was working nearly seven days a week to pay business bills and never had anything left over to contribute to my family. At my clinic's peak, my services included one-on-one occupational therapy, consultation, evaluation, social skills groups, weekly open play sessions, craniosacral therapy, birthday parties, and a parenting group that met multiple times a month all run by me because I could not afford to pay anyone. Needless to say, I was trying to do it all.

I kept telling myself this was normal; this "hustle phase" was what every business needed to go through to get to the light of the life you want to live. And although that may be true at times, my gut was in knots every time I met with my bookkeeper, because while she was supportive and getting me on track to be in the black and paying down debt, she inquired every month, "How will you make more next month to have a profitable business?" What appeared successful from the outside was slowly breaking me down in the form of anxiety, depression, and chronically feeling like I was letting my family down.

Yet through it all, I remained part of Sister Circle, because it was the only positive part of business ownership at that point. I was consistently reminded through the Sister Circle community that while there are seasons of growth to endure, ultimately my business should serve me and my family first. I realized through therapy, self-reflection, and lots of difficult conversations that I was chasing other people's versions of success rather than giving myself time to reflect on what I really wanted from my business.

When I finally opened up about feeling trapped by the rapid growth of Honeybee OT, my husband and I made a plan to pivot from always hustling to finding harmony in my life and business. I instead focused on finding balance and joy in my business again, and I'm still pivoting. I know now that I am at least growing in a way that is more sustainable for me and my family. I can say with confidence that I am now leaning into my intuition and am on my own journey of soul-preneurship and growing in a way that feels aligned with my new definition of success.

Part 3:

Weathering the Storms

"Plants do not only grow in the fresh soil of early spring's rolling green fields, as they receive the right amount of sunshine and rain. They also grow underwater, in the dark, in winter, in the desert. They grow in places most would never think to look. Not all growth happens at one time of year or in one stage of life."

— *Morgan Harper Nichols*

Chapter 7:

Hindsight Is 2020

Jumping Into Action Fast

It was early March 2020 when we started to hear rumblings about COVID and the word *pandemic* came into our vocabulary. Luckily for me, my mentor was jumping into action to have us all create a plan in case we had to close.

What would that look like? How could we continue to serve our members virtually? *Ding, ding, ding*—you guessed it: We'd utilize our on-demand website, which I'd just had my intern build, and live-streaming, which I had done the previous winter while our studio build-out was being finished. By this point in your small business journey, I'm sure you've started to connect the dots to see how meeting challenges and getting creative in one season can serve you so much in another season.

I am proud to say I was as prepared as I could have possibly been. I spent that weekend prior to closing at our friends' house in Minnesota, and we were talking about how crazy it would be if I had to close my studio. As we drove home at the end of the weekend, the media became louder and scarier about the coronavirus. I made the executive decision to hold classes on Monday, March 17, then temporarily close for two weeks, which is what we were told would help stop the spread.

I created an entire live-stream schedule with my staff, who would come in one at a time so we could teach our members on Zoom. We kept our regular five a.m. and five p.m. schedule so our members could have even just an inkling of normalcy and consistency so they wouldn't lose their entire routine for what we thought would be a short period.

We rented out some dumbbells, and I gave my team equipment to use if they had to stream from home. Looking back, that was the last I saw of some of our members, and I had no idea it was the beginning of the end of my first business as I knew it.

I jumped into action so fast, leading from a place of calm even though I had no idea what was happening. I knew I needed to be a light for so many and share my hope and optimism through our classes. Our software didn't have the capacity for live-streaming at the time, so I was sending out individual Zoom links to members before every single class. It was exhausting! I had nightmares that I forgot to send a Zoom link for a five a.m. class.

What we were told would be two weeks to slow the spread turned out to be three months of closure, but we made the most of them. While many people were enjoying the time at home to unplug, rejuvenate, take up new hobbies, and make new routines, I was working overtime again, running on adrenaline and caffeine.

We did equipment orders that I personally delivered to members, and we added new prerecorded classes to the library daily. And the *tech*. I cannot even begin to tell you how difficult it was to navigate all the right audio and video equipment. I spent thousands of dollars and hundreds of hours trying to figure out how to capture the right sound and clear video so our members could stay engaged through Zoom. We did everything possible and whatever we had to do to keep the business going.

It was hard to stay positive and optimistic. This was supposed to be my big year of breakthroughs. One day, I sat and cried as my weekly chakra yoga class left my Zoom window. There I was, alone, in this massive empty studio that I owed a fortune on, and I had no idea when I'd see my members again. Just weeks prior, this room had been packed. The energy buzzing in the studio was everything I had hoped for when I decided to open. But everything had changed, and now it felt so lonely and unfair.

After three months of being closed to in-person business, I was getting nervous going into summer. Summer is already the hardest for gyms and studios, and I knew that if we could only live-stream, we wouldn't make it to reopen for fall. So I attempted to rally all our local gyms and studios to write a letter to the governor, asking to be allowed to open safely. Heck, I even wrote an entire twenty-page reopening manual that ensured safe classes would be held inside and out.

Many businesses and fellow yoga studios and gyms did nothing other than close, and they lost months' worth of revenue. That simply was not an option for me. Plus, I was used to being in survival mode, which fortunately served me. Some studios had just started live-streaming months after we'd already built our online platform and were preparing to reopen. There is something to be said for jumping into action fast to accommodate your clients. I know ours appreciated it greatly during such a scary and uncertain time!

Growth Lessons

Always stay innovative, looking out and ahead to what is coming. And don't be afraid to try new things. Always trust your gut when a new idea comes to you, even when it doesn't make sense to others. It might be coming to you for a reason at just the right time. As an entrepreneur, it's important to be able to make decisions quickly from a place of facts and not fear. Don't sit in indecision too long, especially when it could cost you your business.

While I have always embraced innovation, it doesn't always come easy. Especially when it's forced on you like it was forced on so many during the pandemic. This is why I teach small business owners to always stay open to new ideas and new strategies and to ultimately embrace change. You just never know when it will serve you—especially in a season of weathering storms.

Staying True to Your Values

Finally, in June 2020, we reopened for in-person instruction and kept our class size to ten people. We spaced people out and wiped down all the equipment between people and classes. But, of course, there was one issue that had everyone divided: masks. I knew each of my members personally, and I knew there were going to be people who didn't want to wear a mask and people who did. That put every business owner in a horrible lose-lose situation no matter what they chose to do.

Per usual, I decided to go with my gut, which was telling me that I needed to be consistent in my philosophy: I will never force you to do anything and will always give options. In a workout, I'll never make you do burpees. I'll give you about a million options, and you can pick what works for you that day. Same thing in yoga: I will never force you into a yoga pose. I'll show you options, and you can explore what works for your body. Well, I approached masks the same way because many people already have a hard enough time breathing while doing heavy exercise, and it honestly felt like a liability to force people to cover their airflow during intense exercise—a risk I wasn't willing to take on as a business. (Remember, I'd just gone through an ugly year of a lawsuit, and I never wanted to have that experience ever again!)

Therefore, if you wanted to wear a mask, you could.

If you didn't want to wear a mask, you didn't have to.

I left it up to my clients to choose what made them most comfortable. And if they were uncomfortable being in person without a mask, we *live*-streamed every single in-person class and offered all our pre-recorded videos in our on-demand library.

I felt like I was meeting everyone where they were at. But, of course, you can never make everyone happy, and these were scary times for all. So there wasn't an easy answer or decision to make. I couldn't please everyone. For the first time, I felt like I was disappointing so many by simply trying to accommodate and be inclusive to all. If you're a people pleaser like me, you know that this weighed very heavily on me.

And, of course, this happened when I was trying to enjoy planning my wedding. I had to endure everyone's opinions on whether it was safe to have a wedding in 2020. I was also told that we were selfish to continue to follow through with ours.

In fact, in the summer of 2020, I made a post on social media as a message to those planning their weddings that year, hoping to bring light to just how awful everyone's opinions were in the wedding planning process. At first, it was very well-received. People were commenting, "Exactly how I feel," and "Encompassed my feelings perfectly." Friends and family members sent it to brides, hoping to bring some consolation during a difficult time.

Then, like what happens with all viral posts, the trolls came. "What kind of selfish person holds their wedding during a pandemic, grandma killer!" "Plague rat!" "Is this even a real person?"

Obviously, I am a real person. And I have a fairly thick skin when it comes to haters on the internet who don't know me personally. But reading through the hateful comments started to get to me. Then these people started going after my business, and I was afraid they would attempt to destroy my reputation. I deleted the post quickly. But the message was loud and *clear*: If you hold your wedding this year, it is controversial, and some people will think less of you. Just like how you opened your business back up during the pandemic and some people were upset.

I thought 2019 was hard. Well, 2020 brought so many new challenges I had never faced before as a leader and business owner. It took knowing and trusting my gut well to lead with integrity and my own core values during hard times. People were on edge, and if anyone disagreed with them, they were willing to ruin that person's livelihood, business, or reputation. It was one of the most challenging times I've ever faced as a small business owner.

I thought long and hard about reopening my business and had to remind myself that the opinions of people who were mad about it weren't paying my bills. They didn't have to magically come up with $10,000 a month to break even. So, while it hurt me to see their opinion of me change rather quickly, I had a lot riding on me as I tried to find a way forward to do business as normal.

Growth Lessons

As a small business owner, you will be challenged many times to practice what you preach and be consistent in the face of criticism and adversity. That is why it's so important to know your core values, personally and professionally, and look to them when leading during difficult times. Use those values as your guiding light, and don't be afraid to go against the grain.

If you're a people pleaser, small business ownership will confront your desire to be liked. Instead, focus on being respected. Respect is earned by standing up for your values and beliefs, especially when you're standing alone. You'll be glad you followed your own path instead of conforming to the crowd because you can never make everyone happy anyway. At least you can look back, knowing that you stayed true to yourself. Remember the quote about the man in the arena? Don't take anyone's criticism to heart, especially when they're not the one taking the hits or paying your bills.

Finding Silver Linings

Nothing was normal about 2020. But even during that insanely hard year for business, I continued to look for glimmers of light to keep me going.

Ben and I were planning to save and purchase a house after our wedding that fall. My sister, Cathryn, is a local real estate agent, and I always saw the new home listings she posted or reshared. I loved looking through the houses that came onto the market, just dreaming of the day we'd be able to get out of our tiny apartment and purchase a home of our own.

In June 2020, I saw a house posted that was within what I considered our price range—low—and it actually looked nice! I followed my gut, per usual, and messaged Cathryn to see if she thought we could take a look at it. We got a showing scheduled that day. The moment we walked into the house, I knew it would be ours. Hello again, intuition.

Ben and I walked around to explore the house, already knowing we loved it.

"Well, what's the next step?" I asked.

"To write an offer, you're going to need to be preapproved," Cathryn said.

I replied, "Okay, great. Let's do it!"

Within twenty-four hours, we were preapproved for the home. Cathryn wrote a fantastic offer for us, and within forty-eight hours, we had an offer accepted and were about to become homeowners.

Wow, that was fast. But just like when I walked into my studio space—when you know, you know. And I just knew it was going to be the home where we would build our family. We moved into our beautiful, charming one-and-a-half-story 1920s house in August 2020. And, of course, I got to work painting every room and making it ours immediately. It was one of the best parts of that year. Plus, it was perfect timing because we'd be able to put all our wedding gifts into our brand-new home to help us make it our own.

As the pandemic year continued on, I kept planning for our wedding. Despite the uncomfortable and awkward conversations I continued to have with people who weren't sure if they could make it or if they felt it was safe enough, I thoroughly enjoyed the entire planning process. I love planning parties, and this was one of the most important parties I could ever plan! I wanted it to have all the autumn vintage vibes, so the color palette was dark teal, burnt orange, mustard yellow, maroon, and champagne.

Considering we'd just unexpectedly bought a house and my business future was very uncertain, I was the queen of balling on a budget when it came to wedding planning. I collected vintage candlestick holders, centerpieces, and decor from rummage sales, antique shops, and Facebook Marketplace. I made my own flower bouquets, which now reside in my home as decor. Needless to say, we kept it low-cost but made it classy and beautiful.

The day of our wedding finally came, and, despite all the last-minute cancellations from guests, it was the perfect day! While I originally thought it would be snowing on our wedding day, we lucked out with a seventy-degree day of sunshine in November and the most beautiful autumn sunset. It was perfect. I wish I could live it all over again.

The silver lining of all the cancellations was that we decided to live-stream the wedding and now have the recording to look back on. Everything really does work out the way it's supposed to.

We were on a wedding high, which is why I'm so glad we planned a mini-moon road trip to South Dakota the week following the wedding. I can't imagine going back to work after such an amazing weekend. My team covered all the classes and back-end work for the week, and we enjoyed a week of hiking, exploring, and spending time as newlyweds.

Our ideal honeymoon would have been flying to a tropical island somewhere, but with all the COVID restrictions, we decided we didn't want that to ruin our trip. So we decided to hold off on our dream honeymoon until when we could travel without any restrictions.

As we were heading back from South Dakota, Ben pointed to a post on his phone and said, "Look, husky puppies for sale back home!"

Um, what?

Ben had wanted a Siberian husky for as long as I'd known him. He grew up with huskies and had always wanted a dog. We knew having a husky in an apartment without a yard to run around and play in wouldn't be fair to the dog. So we'd wanted to wait until we bought a house with a yard.

Well, it just so happened that the house we'd bought already had a fenced-in yard. So, when we moved in, Ben had said, "Can we get a dog now?" And I'd responded, "Not until after the wedding!" I was half thinking he'd forget about it. Well, he did *not* forget. Not even a week after our wedding—and not even home from our mini-moon—he was sending me pictures of husky puppies in our area.

To appease him, I said I would go look at them when we got back. So, the day after we got back from our trip, we drove forty-five minutes to "look" at husky puppies. Still, to this day, he says he knew I would be suckered in if I just saw them. And he's right. I was.

Growing up, I never had a dog. The closest pet I ever had was a rabbit named Gracie, and she lived outside because my mom and sister were allergic. So, to say I wasn't a dog person is a bit of an understatement.

But this one little black-and-white puppy with the biggest blue eyes captured our hearts. She wasn't the least bit shy and was rather playful with us. We ended up leaving that night with our first little baby. I held her all the way home as she made little squealing noises. Halfway through the ride home, we stopped at Farm and Fleet to buy her the smallest collar, a leash, food, toys, and a dog bed.

When we got home, she was crawling all over us and running around the house. I had no idea what I was doing as a newly proclaimed dog mom, but I sure did fall in love with her that night. We decided to name her Yuka, which means "brightest star" in Inuit.

I never realized until I wrote this chapter that she was the brightest star in my whole life that year. Buying a home gave us roots to plant our new family, and celebrating our marriage with family and friends was filled with joy. But both were fleeting moments in time that soon became memories.

Yuka brought us so much more. She brought laughter to everyone around us, as I took her everywhere I went, from the studio to my parents' home and to friends' houses and everywhere I went out and about. Her funny faces and playful personality were always the light we needed. She gave me something positive to care about more than my business and something to focus on outside work.

Our daily morning walks became a ritual. Rain or snow, we'd bundle up to get outside together, and it's something I look forward to and treasure to this day. She taught me to be present in the moment like dogs always are. To not worry so much about the future and be playful and curious right here and now.

Even though hindsight is always 20/20, I'd still live that year all over again. Despite all the hardships that 2020 brought, there were so many silver linings and glimmers of goodness, but it took intentionality to search for them. Yuka was the brightest star in a year of darkness and continued to be into my most difficult season ahead of me.

Growth Lessons

Sometimes, business is thriving. And other times, you are just surviving. It's all normal. Business ebbs and flows in seasons and cycles. Business and life are full of highs and lows, valleys and mountaintops. You must learn to ride the waves without getting too high or too low along the way. While it takes intentionality to search for the light in your darkest days, when you do, there are always glimmers of hope and good things that you can be grateful for. See your struggles and suffering as a reminder that you're very much alive and trying. There are always better days ahead.

Embracing Your Struggles

Ben and I got into running with Yuka, and it became a fun family challenge. Yes, I—the long-time, self-proclaimed hater of running— had found some sliver of enjoyment in the challenge of it. We started consistently running together once per week, and I'll admit—it grew on me.

Running is physically challenging. But, of course, what I found inspiring were the life metaphors and epiphanies I had while running. It's almost like the act itself is so awful that I get deep into my thoughts and am hyper-aware of my inner dialogue, like the negotiating I would do to not quit every two minutes.

The more consistently we ran, the more my stamina and endurance noticeably improved, which was encouraging. On one of the hottest, most humid days of summer, we ran up to the top of what we call "bluffs" here in the Coulee Region. These bluffs were formed by glaciers thousands of years ago and created the "Driftless region." Picture a small mountain covered with trees and trails for hiking, biking, and running. They are breathtaking features of where we live and a staple in our community.

So, as we were running up this bluff, I was starting to feel nauseous because it was so dang hot. Plus, this run was legitimately hard. Even Yuka, who usually pulls me up all the hills, was struggling. We finally got to the top, and I puked on the side of the road.

"Okay, we're halfway!" Ben said.

Now we had to make the descent back down, which you'd think would be easier, but I'm not so sure it was. On the whole way back down the bluff, I could feel my body getting chills, which I thought was so weird, considering how hot it was. Then it dawned on me: My body was working overtime to cool myself down.

I fought hard with myself in my head the whole way back. Maybe I should walk. Maybe I should stop. I think I'm going to puke again. When is this trail over? Why does this feel so hard? I shouldn't have eaten so close to running . . . Okay, I can do this. Just keep going.

The dialogue continued on and on and on. Finally, I knew where we were on the trail, and I knew we were on the homestretch. My mind flashed to how grateful I am for my health and how limited our time is here on this Earth. I said to myself, *If I'm alive, I better be moving!* Then I pushed through to the finish line. It was an awesome feeling. I mean, the endorphin rush from running is a *real* thing. I felt it after finishing five miles that day up the bluff and back down on one of the hottest days of the summer.

On the card ride back home, I said to Ben, "Man, that really sucked. That was pure struggle."

His response is something I'll never forget. He replied, "Suffering means you're alive."

Ain't that the truth. To suffer is part of the human experience. The dictionary definition of suffering is: "the state of undergoing pain, distress, or hardship." But here's the epiphany: Your pain, distress, or hardship builds your resiliency. If you suffer on a run or in exercise, you gain endurance, strength, and mental resilience. If you suffer in business and in life, you can use that experience to build strength, courage, and resiliency as well.

But if you never, ever suffer, how can you build your resiliency muscles?

Most of us say we would like to breeze through life without suffering. Yet how boring would it be if we never had any obstacles to overcome? If we never had opportunities to prove to ourselves that we can overcome anything?

What's important is realizing that suffering solely to suffer leads to wasted time and energy. But using your experience of suffering and struggling through something for the *better* is where it becomes a meaningful part of your story.

Now, there is a nuance when it comes to struggling and suffering, and it's something I've had to become aware of in my own story. While these experiences have their place in your journey of overcoming, you don't want to live in a state of suffering, struggle, and scarcity just so you feel like you deserve your success and happiness. It's like taking all things in moderation: When we embrace our struggles, they can serve us.

Oftentimes, we want to avoid the struggles and suffering. But we learn the most and feel the most alive through those experiences— like running up a bluff on a hot day. We can appreciate it after the fact.

So, where are you trying to avoid the struggles or the hard work and, therefore, avoiding the satisfaction that comes from trying, struggling, maybe even failing, and getting back up again?

While my small business journey took me through many seasons of struggle and suffering, I continued to find the purpose in my pain and search for the light amidst the darkness. This mindset of resiliency that I gained through my physical, mental, emotional, and business feats continued to serve me into my hardest season of business yet . . .

Growth Lessons

It is so important to learn to embrace your success and struggles, then ultimately enjoy the process of your small business journey. Every time you reach a goal, celebrate how far you've come before you set a new one. Embrace each milestone along the way. After all, struggles mean you are alive and trying. Without them, your business journey and story would be so boring. Seek out new challenges in your business to flex your resiliency muscle because you never know when you'll need it.

I'm so very grateful that I learned mental and physical resiliency during my MMA days and the years in my business prior to the pandemic. I can't imagine COVID being my first big challenge. By weathering all my previous storms, I gained experiences that gave me confidence that I could make it through that storm.

Chapter Reflections

Reflection Questions:

❖ What is a new, innovative strategy or change you'd like to make in your business? What is stopping you from trying it? How could it bring positive change on the other side of implementation?

❖ What are your personal and business core values? Has there been a time when you were tested and needed to rely on them to make a hard decision?

❖ What are the silver linings in your own storms of small business ownership? Where did you search for glimmers of hope for better days?

❖ Where and how have you had to flex your resiliency muscles to get through a hard season?

Intentional Action:

• New Small Business Owner: There will be storms along your journey and people in your path who test you and question your integrity. If you haven't already, write down your personal and business core values. Post your business values on your website and your personal values in your office, then refer to them often—especially amidst your storms. Stay true to yourself and continue to build your muscle of resilience. And always, always, always take the high road. You never know when life will come full circle.

- Seasoned Small Business Owner: Use the storms along your journey as an opportunity to try something new. Is there a change or innovation you've been interested in implementing? Why not give it a go—even on a small scale? Remember, always beta test! Check in with the personal and business core values you wrote initially. Do they still resonate? Maybe it's time to do a little updating based on where you and your business have evolved to. Post them and share about them everywhere you can. People love to see how you are evolving, so take them along for the journey. And *please* take some time to celebrate how far you've come. Like, seriously *celebrate*. Mark your calendar right now for a day to take yourself somewhere, treat yourself, or throw a party with your friends, family, or fellow small business sisters. It doesn't have to cost anything. Maybe it's just a day off work or a hike. I love celebrating with a coffee date with myself, a good book, and maybe a little boutique shopping for a bright-colored blazer. Whatever your jam is, just make it happen.

First family photo in our new home with our new puppy, Yuka (2020)

Chapter 8:

Some People Are a Season for a Reason

Not Everyone Who Starts with You Will Stay with You

This chapter is probably the hardest to write because it's one of the most painful lessons to learn in life and, especially, business. You will meet so many people along your entrepreneurial journey and in your life. And some people are a season for a reason.

In my early years of business ownership, it was rare for me to gain a new client or add a team member who was short-lived. A lot of the people who helped me grow my studio in the early years supported me wholeheartedly, and I naively thought they would support me forever, especially on my growth journey!

I learned the hard way in my first studio expansion that not everyone was going to follow me to my new space. That hurt. I had built a lot of personal relationships and considered those people friends. But, for whatever reason, this next chapter of my business was just not for them. I tried not to let it get me down. Instead, I focused on the people who were still there and were excited about it.

As I continued to grow and expand my team, I was very selective about who I brought into my dream. I had a few bad hiring judgment calls over the years. One in particular tried to take my clients with her when she left. But overall, I was fortunate to have good people on my team for the majority of the decade I spent building the business, up until COVID.

In my experience, and maybe in yours too, the pandemic sent a lot of people over the edge and created loss in so many ways for so many. I lost members who weren't ready to come back in person, had built their own home routines, or became disengaged and stopped showing up altogether. But I also lost many team members as we tried to navigate this new normal.

We were all overworked. Stressed. Burned out on life and pivoting. I admit that expecting my team of instructors to be great group fitness and yoga instructors in person and now also accommodate everyone's needs and preferences virtually—not to mention learn new technology—was overwhelming. I myself was completely overwhelmed and, quite honestly, very frustrated. It was the only way we could stay in business. But even though we all understood that it was the only way we could keep going, it didn't make it any easier.

At the end of the day, people's lives had changed. Our daily routines were completely different. Many people started working from home and even leaving home less and less. Life and priorities shifted. What was once a fun side gig for my team became more stressful. There was a lot of pressure to get the technology right and show up with energy, even if there was one person in the room and five on Zoom. Teaching to black boxes on a screen wasn't fun, and the joy and energy of group fitness and a packed room felt like a dream of the past.

It was the hardest season in my entrepreneurial journey, and I was struggling to keep it together. That didn't make it easier when people started leaving.

One day, yet another team member had decided to quit. It felt like another knife to the heart. What was I doing wrong? Couldn't they see that I was trying my best to recover from COVID? Couldn't they see that I was mentally and financially struggling? Couldn't they see how hard I was working to get us back to normal? The most painful losses were friends and team members who had been part of the business since the early days. It's always the most painful when it's the people you least expect to leave you, especially in your darkest days.

I was going deeper into my darkest valley at this point, and I could feel the tears welling in my eyes and the pit growing in my stomach as I thought, *Well, now I will be covering their classes and having to start over training someone else. I feel like the worst leader and business owner ever.*

Regardless, the show had to go on. I put on a smile and taught class, pretending everything was all good, per usual. I can't tell you how many times I had to fake my way through those years of pain, loss, and struggle. While I couldn't fake my way forever, it did help me keep moving forward when I otherwise would have spiraled.

I reached out to my mentor for encouragement and advice because I felt like I was reaching my breaking point. During class one day, she left me a voicemail, giving me consolation and words I'll never forget: "This is one of the most painful parts of the entrepreneurial journey . . . is recognizing that some of the people that helped you to build the business will not be there to help you build it going forward. A lot of times, it's not about you. People just move on. But when this happens, God has always brought me somebody new that I didn't even know I needed, so hang in there."

Deep breaths. My eyes welled up again as I got into my car to drive home after my longest day of teaching. A thought came to me on the drive as I pondered why this kept happening to me: *Some people are a season for a reason. Some people stay forever.*

I could sit in sadness and sulk about all the people I'd lost in the last decade—friends, family, team members, and clients. It didn't do me any good to try to think about what I did wrong or why we drifted apart. When we lose people, it often has nothing to do with us. Life priorities change and people change. Heck, I changed a lot. And that's all part of the journey.

At the end of the day, I'm still grateful for those people—the lessons learned, the memories made, and the contributions they made to my life for the season they were present for. I'd love to say that losing people in business and in life gets easier over time. But I think that if you really care about people, that statement is simply not true.

Along the journey, I learned to create more boundaries between business and friendships to guard my heart from repeating the same mistakes I made as a young entrepreneur. But I don't think that hurt ever fully goes away. We still have scars, especially from the painful losses of people. But I will say that we get thicker armor.

This is also a reminder that doing business with friends and family can be difficult. In my early years, I treated my staff more as friends than employees, which made it challenging when it came to growing the business, giving feedback, and, especially, parting ways. When you're starting out, though, it's difficult not to treat your team like friends. This was especially true for me when I was younger than all my staff. I didn't feel like a boss to them. Eventually, I was leading people of many different ages and generations, and it was difficult to meet everyone where they were at.

Leading people is probably one of the hardest challenges you will ever face as a small business owner, and it's usually one you're not prepared for. You might start alone with your idea as a solopreneur. Then you begin to grow and hire people you know (a.k.a. friends and family). Now you have a team to lead, manage, train, and motivate. It's a tough job. And it's even harder when you're forced to lead during unforeseen challenges.

One of my favorite practices was our quarterly team training. These meetings started as opportunities to let everyone get to know each other better and stay up to date on what was coming. But they evolved into days of training, learning, and team bonding we did each quarter. I loved planning fun activities for each one. We usually started with a team workout with our members, followed by a guest speaker, then a brainstorming session for future ideas and promotions. We finished with a fun group activity and sometimes even dinner!

I organized speakers for all areas of the business, from instructional classes to marketing to sales. I felt it was important for us to all learn and grow together in each other's areas of expertise. After all, we were all working toward a shared mission and vision for the business. I used these quarterly training sessions to remind us of our efforts, the progress we were making together, and who we were going to be along the way (core values). And we collectively brainstormed how we would get there together.

The bottom line: I came to learn that nobody will ever care more about your dream than you do—even your most loyal people. Your dream is your dream to protect. It's not their vision! They might be all in on your mission and love everything you stand for, but at the end of the day, your vision is yours for a reason. You have to build the armor, resilience, and drive to move forward whether they are along for the ride or not. But, man, the people who move forward with you? They are your ride-or-dies.

Growth Lessons

Not everyone who starts with you will stay with you. In business, this is a hard lesson to accept and not take personally. Some clients and team members will grow with you. Others will choose not to, and it often has nothing to do with you. Thank them for the season they contributed to and trust that when you bless and release them for your next season, someone amazing is about to step into their place.

While I wholeheartedly believe that the best people who help you grow your business often come to you as clients first, it doesn't mean you should forgo all professionalism. Try your best to maintain boundaries and mutual respect as a business owner and a team member. But this doesn't mean you don't care about them as a person. I've found this takes time and intentional effort. It often must be learned the hard way, but it's nothing you can't handle. At this point in your circle of growth, you've flexed your resiliency muscles and have built some thicker armor. You are stronger than you think!

Find Your Tribe and Love Them Hard

When people start to leave, you'll notice who stays. Those are your people, and you *must* pour into them. I couldn't write this chapter without mentioning the tribe of people who made the entire decade of my first business worth it. They came to be known as the Good Vibes Tribe.

First and foremost, my team. While we had a lot of ups and downs as a team as we weathered many storms, we also made a lot of fun memories. There were early mornings, late nights, dance parties, live sales, team trainings, and hard work. It wasn't always easy, but they made it worth it. I'll never have the words to say just how much it meant to me to have these people sticking it out with me until the very end: my mom, Kelly, Anne, Kerrigan, Alexa, and Courtney. Thank you for supporting me through my darkest days and deepest valleys.

My tribe of members: You have no idea how much you kept me going day in and day out. I believe I never went into a full-on depression because I *had* to get up every day at 4:30 a.m. I had to show up for all of you, whether I had it in me or not. You pulled out the best in me. You loved on me so hard when I felt unworthy of love at all. When I felt like a failure, you always reminded me of how much I made your day and how my classes were the one thing you looked forward to.

My Good Vibes Tribe kept me connected to my why and kept me driving forward when I didn't know how I was going to come up with my next rent payment. When I felt worthless because I had only a few dollars to my name, your "I loved that class choreography today" and "Your class is simply the best part of my day!" filled up my cup to keep going.

While I know I acquired an unhealthy attachment to my worth being wrapped up in making my business my identity, it served me in this season. I needed to feel like the mission mattered because I was barely holding on by a thread, digging my way out of COVID recovery, debt, and looming depression.

I wrote this chapter to remind you that not everyone will stick around for every season and that, while it's painful, you're better for it. While I care about the people I do business with, I was simply a transactional service to some. I get it. They were coming to me for fitness and yoga. To others, I was a friend, mentor, life coach, and teacher. Those are the people I cherish and want to stay connected with to this day. We have to learn to bless and release the rest. Through growing and scaling a business, I learned the hard way to separate my worth from how other people perceived me, what they received from me, or whether they left me.

It's so important to remember that you and your business are not for everyone. When you are in your planting and growing phases, you will often appeal to a larger audience because you are still trying to figure out who exactly your ideal client is. As you continue along your circle of growth, you'll naturally lose some people who aren't meant for you. Remember: a season for a reason. But see it as an opportunity to get laser-focused on who exactly you *are* for.

We often focus on those who leave, blaming ourselves and wondering what we did wrong, when there are people standing right in front of us, happy and eager to stay. Put your attention and energy on them. Those are your people. Love them hard by continuing to show up and tailor your offerings to continue to appeal to them and people like them. Show your tribe why you appreciate them through simple things, like encouragement, compliments, or even client gifts. Throw them a party of appreciation!

This is something we did so well: loving on the tribe of people who stuck around. We threw a VIP party every year for our members that included food, drinks, fun, member-voted awards, goodie bags, giveaways, dance parties, and so much more. We went all out on it, and our clients looked forward to it every year.

I did the same thing to shower my team with fun team outings and bonding time, team trainings, and gifts around the holidays. Sometimes, it could be as simple as telling them, "Great class, you rocked it!" and checking in with them weekly.

By being personal with your people, you will continue to stand out as a business owner because it shows that they are more than just a transaction, dollar sign, or number. I can't tell you how many times people canceled their membership only to come back a few months or years later. So don't burn bridges. You'd be shocked at how relationships can come full circle. That also goes for building your connections.

I can't tell you how many past studio clients referred me to their friends, even if they were no longer attending classes. As I began to start and grow new business ventures, my tribe of people have shown up to support me time and time again. You just might be one of them. *Thank you!*

As I weathered the storms of my small business journey, there were many times when I felt lonely, even though I had great people around me. The weight I carried as the owner was heavy, and I knew I couldn't be the only small business owner experiencing these challenges. I began to feel called to create another type of community outside my Good Vibes Tribe and team—specifically, a community where female small business owners could feel less alone in their experiences.

Growth Lessons

As you grow and evolve your business, it will become clear who you are and are not for and what your ideal client values. Focus your attention and energy not on mourning those who leave but on appreciating and loving the people who stick it out with you through all the highs and lows. Once you know the ideal client you want to attract, market to that specific person. Put it on your website and social media channels. Highlight your current all-star clients and ask them to refer their friends to draw in more just like them. You know the saying: "When you appeal to everyone, you attract no one." Don't be afraid to be specific so the right people will align with you.

As you create your loyal tribe of clients and team members in business, find ways to acknowledge, encourage, and support them through their journey so they want to stay connected with you and refer you to their friends. Whether it's with client gifts, appreciation events, or simple, handwritten notes, find ways to stand out and show your people that you appreciate their business and your relationship with them—because you never know when a connection will come full circle!

Create the Community You Need for the Season You're In

While I had built a strong community with my Good Vibes Tribe of women who loved working out and finding their Zen together, I was craving community among other local small business owners.

I don't know if I would have made it through the first year in that studio space without the More Than Just Great Dancing community that my mentor led. I needed that next-level education, training, and encouragement to get through that nasty lawsuit with my ex-landlord, increase my sales, and grow my team to support the business. It was a saving grace in 2019—and especially when the COVID pandemic hit. While we pivoted online, having this community and my mentor's guiding light through that time was essential. But I was craving a community closer to home.

In the summer of 2021, I was invited to invest in myself again to become a certified coach for the More Than Just Great Dancing community. While I was honored to have this opportunity, it was a big investment. To be honest, I wasn't sure I was worth the investment. What skills could I possibly bring to this community? Even though I had made large gains in my own business, I still felt unmatched when standing next to the veteran coaches. But it's important to know that when your mentor invites you to do something, you should just say *yes!* So I went all in again.

I signed up for an intensive three-day training held locally. I was broke coming out of COVID, and my business was feeling the hit. But I knew that was why I needed to do it. In all honesty, I was looking for something different. I wanted new challenges and personal development. I had no idea how becoming a certified coach for this company would change my entire trajectory. In fact, I'd argue that although it was the most expensive investment I've ever made in a business coaching program, it was the best investment and the most transformational experience I've ever had. Another turning-point moment.

In the first two days, we learned how to develop a topic, create a story sparkline, present effectively, and build a personal brand as a speaker, coach, and writer. Then, on day three, we had to present on stage to the group and receive feedback. Talk about putting yourself out there! But I did it.

This training was a catalyst and a springboard to expanding my skills into speaking, coaching, writing, and podcasting. The teacher and performer in me loved this training. I was able to use my love of being on stage and teaching content I am passionate about with more confidence and grace. It gave me the tools I needed to effectively share my story through speaking, podcasting, and writing this book.

I was asked to lead all kinds of monthly calls for More Than Just Great Dancing on topics like social media, productivity, and work-life balance. I was feeling very fulfilled through the online training, but I knew I needed to push myself further. It was time to hone in on my on-stage speaking skills.

I didn't do what most people would probably do: I didn't seek out other stages to speak on and speak for. Instead, I created my own stage to speak on and a community to come together. That's because it is true: We often create the community we wish we had. When you're looking for opportunities, the best advice I can give you is to create your own. So often, we wait around for people and opportunities to find us. But that rarely ever happens. If you can't find what you're looking for, maybe you're meant to create it—a lesson that continues to come up in my own entrepreneurial journey.

When I looked around for local business experiences to learn from and connect with after the pandemic, there wasn't much in our area. A lot of the in-person groups and experiences had faded during the pandemic and hadn't returned. I was searching for a community of growth-minded female small business owners who got together on a monthly basis to not just chitchat or gossip but talk about real business strategy. And that wasn't something I found offered locally.

I was on the phone with my sister one day and had an idea: "What if we created an experience to bring in business speakers to learn from locally?" So much of the business space felt dominated by men, and we wanted to create a room just for women so they would feel safe, seen, and connected.

Being an innovator and visionary who's full of ideas, I got my sister on board with me. We met at my favorite local coffee shop, Moka, to brainstorm more ideas.

Well, of course I showed up with a full logo idea. Then we came up with the name: Small Business Sister Circle™. Cathryn represented the *C* and moon, and I represented the *S* in the original logo. We prepared to launch our first very small picnic meeting by simply gathering a small group of female small business owners we knew at the time to pitch our idea to.

I knew from the very beginning, though, that this idea would become so much *more* than just a small group of women. But, just like any business, you have to start somewhere. And, as you know, I'm a big proponent of the "start small but dream big" mentality.

So we did just that. We gathered a group of ten small business women we knew for a dreamy picnic and pitched our idea to meet monthly to discuss different business topics. And they loved it! We gathered photos and videos of that picnic to share our vision, and we officially launched the business.

The response we received from that first meeting was overwhelmingly positive. And there was a lot of curiosity. Women asked, "When are you going to do this again?"

So we came up with our next experience: a Sister Circle Social. We also filled that event, and I was already dreaming bigger: "Let's host a small business conference!"

In November 2021, we hosted our very first local Sister Circle Summit and had twenty-five women show up. Again, start small, dream big. My goal was to just keep growing this community organically. So, in 2022, we hosted our second small business summit with fifty people, doubling our attendance. We had lots of different socials, in-person workshops, and online webinars. I even did some one-on-one business coaching.

It was a sampler year that let us try all kinds of offerings and see not only what stuck and sold out but what we enjoyed doing. We were still running our monthly meetings with our original small group, and I knew this could be bigger and create much more impact. Yet I was still running my first business, Zen and Pow Studio, so my time was fairly limited.

In this same year, Cathryn was expecting her second daughter, and since I'd roped her into my original vision for Sister Circle, she gave me full permission to take the business and run with it. And I did just that.

The pop-up events were great, and connecting in the monthly meetings was fun. But I still felt like there was something missing. I saw the opportunity for this community to go deeper and fill a gap in the local business market. Even though we started small with humble beginnings—just like I did with my first business—I had a big vision for what it could become! But as the year went on, I held off on my vision for Sister Circle because my first business kept pulling me back in . . .

Growth Lessons

We all need support and encouragement along our small business journey. Find a community that supports you for the season you're in. If you can't find it, create it for yourself and invite others to join you. If we don't have support from a community, we often don't know what we're missing until we are surrounded by positive, growth-minded, uplifting individuals who understand our struggles and cheer us on in our successes.

We so often think we are the only ones experiencing struggles in business. But that is simply not true. I knew there had to be others like me who were also craving depth in their business relationships and strategy in order to scale sustainably. There is so much research behind why it's important to have in-person community and relationships, especially coming out of the pandemic.

Chapter Reflections

Reflection Questions:

- ❖ Can you recall a relationship that was a season for a reason? What did you gain from going through it? How did you find closure?
- ❖ Who is your ideal client? How can you attract more of them?
- ❖ How can you love on the people who show up for you in business and in life?
- ❖ Where can you seek out a community or build your own so you feel supported in your small business journey?
- ❖ What do you value in a community?

Intentional Action:

- New Small Business Owner: Focus on building personal relationships from the very beginning of your business. Too many people focus on building their social media platforms, which can be a container for building community. But I recommend building in real life. Get crystal clear on who your business is for and who it is not for, then put that in your marketing. The clearer you can be, the more you will continue to attract your ideal client. While you build your loyal tribe of clients, find your tribe of small business sisters to support you along your journey! Whether you want to create your own community, join one in your local area, or join Sister Circle, find somewhere you can go for support that offers what you value in community.

- Seasoned Small Business Owner: You earn the title of a seasoned small business owner after you've lost some people along the way. I don't have to tell you how painful it is to let go of people who have helped you build your business, whether through firing or allowing people to move on. If you haven't found closure in it, what is blocking you? I challenge you to find gratitude. Maybe even write them a thank-you note for all they taught you (for better or for worse). You don't have to mail it. You can even set it on fire! Once you can find some closure, turn all your attention onto everything that has stayed. How can you love on them? Is it through giving them a gift, throwing an exclusive party, or simply asking them to lunch or coffee? Keep pouring into them. They are there for a reason. And I'll give the same advice I gave above: Whether you want to create your own community, join one in your local area, or join Sister Circle, find somewhere you can go for support that offers what you value in community.

The very first Sister Circle conference (2021)

Chapter 9:

Embracing Your Evolution

Embracing New Challenges and Beginnings

I knew by the summer of 2022 that things were not looking good for my fitness and yoga studio business. The COVID recovery grants and funds had run dry, and people were Zoomed out of online live-streams, disconnected, and lacking community.

Personally, I was burned out mentally, physically, and on a soul level. Something had to *give*. And that something was going to need to be big.

I knew it, and it killed me inside to realize that this business and the dream I had been pursuing for the last nine years were actually crushing me. I had tried every possible idea to come back after the pandemic and get out of the red financially. But it just wasn't happening.

It was time to make a massive pivot and get creative . . . but not in the way I had in the past. Something needed to drastically change, and that's where my pivot into real estate came in. My sister had pivoted from direct sales into real estate about six years prior, had made a very successful career in the industry, and loved it.

I was talking with Cathryn on the phone one day that summer while I was doing dishes. Out of nowhere, she said, "Have you ever thought of getting into real estate?"

I laughed and scoffed, saying, "Um, no. Are you kidding?"

"Well, no. I think you'd be really good at it."

"Wait, are you serious? I don't know why you'd think that. I don't know anything about it.

"Well, neither did I when I started. But it's a lot of people skills, and you're relational. You coach and motivate people daily!" she said.

The thoughts in my head were running about a million miles per hour, telling me why I'd never be good at real estate. The main thoughts were: *I am a creative person. Real estate is not creative. It's contracts and legal lingo. No thanks. How boring!*

But that conversation stirred up some curiosity inside me. The conversation continued with my husband and my parents, who were all convinced that I should pursue real estate part-time and at least give it a go. I mean, what did I have to lose at that point? My first business was financially suffering. I needed to pay my bills. And, in complete honesty, I needed a new challenge.

As you know by now, I love challenges. But I was burned out by the same problems, day after day, month after month, year after year . . . I was ready for something different. But I wasn't quite ready to give up my first dream. So I convinced myself I would study for the real estate exam, launch my real estate career, stay at my studio, and use my additional income from commissions to pay my rent each month and try to get ahead again and out of the red.

Lucky for me, my friend and team leader, Sherie, welcomed and encouraged me to join her real estate team. That was the convincing I needed. Working alongside my sister and being mentored by her and Sherie was the only thing that got me to give it a try in the first place. I would have *never* even attempted to get into real estate without their support, mentorship, and belief in me. I still didn't think it was going to be for me, but they had such a strong belief in me. Just as I had done in the past when I didn't quite believe in myself, I borrowed belief from a friend or mentor to take a chance and gave it my all until my own confidence caught up.

My guess is that at this point in your business journey, you've taken chances, pivoted, and made big leaps before you felt ready. Before you had confidence and belief in yourself, maybe someone else did. Does anyone come to mind when you think of how you found the courage to go for it despite the fear of failing? Be sure to thank them when you can and seek out ways to do this for other people. I love being the little whisper in someone's ear, reminding them, "You got this! I believe in you. I'm proud of you." Even when things don't always go as planned, because they rarely ever will, be that source of support for someone else. You never know when you'll need it for yourself.

So there I was in September 2022 when I made the announcement that I was trying something new and getting into real estate. I realized how hard it was going to be to run my studio full-time with my team, learn the real estate industry, host Sister Circle events, and do all of the things . . . But little did I realize that my plan to stay at my studio wouldn't be sustainable.

By October, my heart was heavy because I knew a big decision was coming. I needed to scale back my first business. I was working *extra* hard in a brand-new industry that already presents a big learning curve for those breaking into it. But taking that income to pay my studio rent each month felt like a step backward. I was burning the candle at both ends and was very much burned out. Not to mention, my yoga lights started to flicker again . . . That's all the confirmation I needed to trust my sign and my intuition. And if I was being honest with myself, my passion for my first business had dwindled drastically since the challenges of 2020. I was excited about the potential and possibilities of a fresh start in real estate.

But to admit this felt like failure. Half of me felt like I failed myself, my clients, my team, and my first dream by scaling back. The other half felt like I would be failing my future self by not giving this new venture a chance. It was time to make some hard decisions about pivoting and re-envision what success looked like for me in this new season.

Growth Lessons

If you're a small business owner, chances are you embrace change more than most people. We need new challenges to keep us inspired, excited, and growing in business and in life. With new challenges comes the opportunity to be a beginner again. It's so essential to seek out new ways to learn, grow, and be a beginner again, whether that's trying something new in your business, launching a new business venture altogether, or even taking on a new hobby in your personal life. New challenges bring new perspectives and pivots you may have never found otherwise.

If you identify with the definition of a soul-preneur like I do— an entrepreneur who intentionally builds their business based around their soul purpose and in alignment with their values to make a positive impact on those they serve—your soul purpose will evolve as you do! Be sure to continue to allow yourself space to explore new beginnings even before you feel ready to. Find the people who support your evolution and give you the courage to try something new while cheering you on along the way.

Making Hard Decisions to Pivot and Re-envision

Something had to give. I felt the tug on my heart to make a big, scary decision, but I knew it was the right decision. Isn't it funny how often the right decision is the most difficult to make? It was as painful as ever to let go. I think I grieved the loss of my studio dream and the loss of the younger version of myself for an entire year leading up to it.

I finally built up the courage to text my mentor and landlord: *Can we meet?* She agreed, and I walked into that meeting with the heaviest heart, feeling like I had failed not only myself but her.

We sat down. I showed her and her husband the numbers and said, "I've implemented everything you've taught me. I've been tracking everything. The numbers don't add up. Being here doesn't make sense anymore. We've lost so many people in person, and the space is much larger than we need."

At this point, I had been struggling to make ends meet for four years and was almost three months behind in rent. I felt awful about how deep I was spiraling, knowing I couldn't possibly work any harder.

"We don't want you to go any deeper into debt. We want the best for you," she said.

"As much as I love being here, I think it's time for me to leave," I said through teary eyes. I was just trying to hold it all together.

They wholeheartedly agreed and supported me. Then they asked me when I wanted to be done.

Just like that, I felt the weight lift off me. What a feeling of freedom. I hadn't expected that. I hadn't thought about when I wanted to be done because it didn't feel like a possibility. I had spent so many years living in a dark tunnel with no end in sight. Then, with one simple phrase, I saw a flicker of a light . . .

"End of November?" I said. "I want to take December off." I restated, "I *need* to take December off."

Done. Just like that. I had an end date. I can still feel the relief of that meeting. That one day completely changed my trajectory—another turning point—because I had the courage to sit down and have one of the hardest conversations I'd experienced so far on my small business journey.

When I stood up to leave, my mentor hugged me and said, "In a year, you'll look back and tell me this was the best decision you ever made."

She was right.

I spent the next month in creation mode. I finally had some life inside me to get creative again. Now that I had such a heavy weight lifted, thanks to that initial decision, everything just started to fall into place. It's funny how that works.

Once you make the hard decision that your gut is telling you to make, the floodgates open with opportunities and possibilities!

I re-envisioned my first business into a pop-up studio and rented my friend Emilene's beautiful space inside Greenhouse for my yoga and sculpt classes. As fate would have it, I went back to my original studio at Iron Works for my fitness and kickboxing classes. Remember how I said you never know when something will come full circle?

I made the announcement to my team, clients, and larger community. Then, yes, I took December off to fill up my cup again and take a much-needed break from teaching classes.

I was able to sell most of my equipment and furniture to pay off the three months of rent I owed, but my business loan was still sitting around $100,000. It was a sunk cost at that point, though. I knew I was better off walking away and paying it off through whatever other means possible than trying to recover my losses.

My guess is that at this point of weathering storms in your small business, you've had to make hard decisions to cut your losses—time, money, and energy spent—to move down a path that's more aligned with your future. It's painful but so worth it. The relief you feel when you make that hard decision will tell you everything you need to know about whether it was the right decision.

Even though I was grieving, I felt a deep relief. There was a light flickering at the end of the tunnel I had been traveling in for so long, and that little flicker kept guiding me through the darkness.

On my thirtieth birthday, I turned in the keys to that studio space that held so many deep memories and life lessons, then turned a new page into a new decade of my life.

Growth Lessons

Trust your gut and know when it's time to pivot and re-envision your business in a way that will more positively impact your life. Every few years in business, you have to make hard decisions, oftentimes leaving a sunk cost behind to pivot your business to suit the season you're in. Every successful business owner I've ever learned from has memories and lessons learned of cutting their losses on something that didn't work out and taking the higher road to something new.

Learn to embrace your evolution. It makes sense that your dreams will evolve as you do. Listen to your intuition to know when it's time to make a hard decision to pivot and have fun creating something new!

Listen to Your Gut to Launch Something New

This was not exactly where I thought I'd be at age thirty.

I thought I'd have kids, a stable business, and more money in my savings. I thought I'd be able to travel and soak up the rewards of my decade of soul-preneurship.

Instead, I felt like I was starting over. And in many ways, I was.

I took December off, scaled back my first business, and launched my real estate career. You'd think that would be enough change for this new thirty-year-old. But I still had a nagging tug on my heart to build something deeper with Small Business Sister Circle.

I had been teaching and preaching collaboration over competition to Sister Circle since the beginning. I'd also been practicing it myself in business. The research on why we need community was continuing to show up for me. Having community and social relationships is the number-one predictor of happiness. But how you belong to your community and tap into it with collaboration is also the deeper reason for needing it. Because here's the thing: Communities exist without collaboration, but collaboration doesn't exist unless you tap into your communities.

How many groups are you a part of online or in real life that you barely show up for? We say we want more depth, more connection, and more genuine relationships. But is that true based on our participation? I knew I wouldn't feel like part of a community unless I showed up and participated in monthly meetings and in-person events. I knew I'd need to make an honest effort to build real relationships. That was the vision I had for Sister Circle and why I knew I needed to grow it to its full potential.

To this day, I cannot explain why I had that vision other than it was a true God calling to pursue the goal I had for this business from the very beginning: to build it into a monthly membership.

Call me crazy because I'm sure I looked like it! I felt like my first business had just failed. Who the heck was I to lead and teach other small business owners how to be successful? And why did I need to launch another membership after I'd just scaled back my first membership business? What was wrong with me? Why did I need to have my hands in so many different things? Why couldn't I just be "normal" and focus on *one* thing?

Have you ever had in your gut a feeling you needed to follow that didn't make sense to anyone else—maybe not even you? Maybe you're a multi-passion soul-preneur like me and have a deep desire to pursue multiple business ventures. Maybe you look a little insane to most people. Just know that I see you and feel you.

I tuned out the negative thoughts and pursued the idea anyway. I mapped it out. And I got smart and strategic about it this time. I wasn't making any decisions on a whim like I did in my first business.

That's the difference I've seen in entrepreneurs who pursue many different things. They still need to be strategic about it. They make sure it all makes sense and leads to their larger purpose. And they put systems in place so they can manage multiple businesses well. Nobody wants to be that business owner who jumps from one business and idea to another without fully committing to anything. Do one thing well, slowly add in another, and make sure you are able to show up as your best self in what you're pursuing.

With the help of my friend and true sales genius, Alana, I came up with a membership model to offer at my end-of-the-year Sister Circle Social in December. I was so excited to launch it! I felt so good about it.

The event was packed, and it went amazing. I shared the new Sister Circle Membership with the room of female small business owners. Then I explained that I'd created it just for them and told them it was ready to launch for January 2023.

And it was crickets . . . other than member number one, who'd signed up that evening. (I am forever grateful for her—thank you, Kristen!) If she hadn't committed, I probably would have scrapped the idea altogether and thrown it away, never to revisit it again.

Needless to say, I was discouraged when I got home. That response was the proof I needed that this membership hadn't been worth creating and nobody wanted it. It would have made sense to quit on the idea right then and there. But with some encouragement from Alana, I tweaked it from an annual commitment to a quarterly membership and decided to keep trying.

My goal was fifteen founding members. I told myself that if I didn't get those fifteen before we launched in January, I wasn't going to do it.

Well, after some marketing (hello—you can't put an offer out there once and expect that to be it), I got more specific about the small business owners we were looking to appeal to. And we kicked off January 2023 with not fifteen but eighteen founding members. It was decided: I was launching the Sister Circle Membership!

When something is a calling on your heart, it's your responsibility to bring it to life. It doesn't mean it's going to become your grand vision right away, though. I can't tell you how many times I've thought something was a great idea, only to get crickets when I launched it into the world. An unenthusiastic response doesn't necessarily mean your idea isn't going to work or that it's a bad idea. Maybe it just needs some tweaking or more marketing to get it out there.

Growth Lessons

Not every idea you have for your business is going to be a slam dunk. But some ideas are worth pursuing, even if the response is not what you hoped for from the beginning. Remember, start small and dream big! It often takes gathering feedback, going back to the drawing board, and figuring out a new way to relaunch it. Or just marketing it *more*. You can't expect to put something out into the world once and have it be a bestseller. You have to keep talking about it, sculpting it into what people want, and trying again. Follow your intuition, even when it doesn't always make sense to others or to you. You may be onto something new, and it may take some time for others to catch onto it.

Chapter Reflections

Reflection Questions:

❖ Where can you be a beginner again—in business or in life—to gain new perspectives?

❖ Think back to a big pivot or hard decision you made. How did trusting your gut to make that change work out for you?

❖ Do you currently feel a nudge to make a hard decision or big pivot? What is stopping you from doing so?

❖ Have you ever had to leave a sunk cost behind? Why? And how did it serve you?

❖ Do you have a nudge to try something new but are unsure of what the response would be? How can you start small, gather feedback, and adapt it as you go?

Intentional Action:

• New Small Business Owner: You have already tackled the challenge of becoming a beginner again at this whole business owner thing. Kudos to you for following your nudge! Maybe you're already feeling like you need to pivot from your original idea for a product or service. That's normal. Continue to pivot and evolve as you figure out what you want your business to be so you can avoid having to make some of the hard decisions later. But honestly, there will always be hard decisions and pivots in business, so your best bet is to become flexible and adaptable. Learn to love your evolution.

- Seasoned Small Business Owner: Well, you're no longer a beginner business owner, but maybe you need to try something new, pivot, or even make a hard decision for your next evolution—even if it means leaving behind a sunk cost because it's just not working. Take some time to get quiet and step out of the hustle of your day-to-day so you can really *hear* your intuition. What is your gut saying you need to do? Test out that decision and dream again. What would it look like to re-envision your business? Give yourself permission to *change*. We get so used to doing what we normally do and what people expect of us. It can be scary to pivot or make a hard decision when we feel like we are disappointing others. Embrace the unknown of being a beginner again and get excited about your next evolution. Write down everything you want your business and life to look and feel like. Then, step by step, make it happen!

One of my favorite memories of Zen and Pow at our
Outdoor DJ Dance Party (2022)

Small Business Sister Story: Emilene Heiderscheit

Weathering the Storms and Finding Light

Small business ownership isn't for the faint of heart—trust me, I know. I once believed that aligning with God's purpose would banish fear. My mission was to give back by spreading love, healing, and showing compassion, trusting that every miracle in my life was a promise to pay it forward. But I soon learned that a good heart and kind intentions don't always protect you from life's hardships, disguised as your teacher.

When COVID-19 hit, our community-driven business—only six months old—was abruptly shut down. Over the next five years, I faced heartbreak, betrayal, and the exhausting process of rebuilding my team and relationships, even with those I once considered close friends. I encountered narcissism and learned the hard way. Even with integrity and honesty, honoring core values, sometimes leave you feeling disposable still. Even simple tasks like asking for help became challenges, forcing me to seek clarity and forgiveness for both myself and those around me.

In the midst of these storms, I realized that true autonomy begins with God. Instead of seeking external validation, I learned to look inward and cultivate resilience. It was during these trying times that Stephanie entered my life—a bright light arriving at the perfect moment. Her insights and unwavering authenticity reminded me of the importance of staying true to my core values, even when others don't understand. As a soul-preneur who wears her heart on her sleeve, I strive to keep relationships that align with my truth—just as I do with my children, my number one priority.

Stephanie became the non-biased coach and friend I desperately needed. Her guidance—like a clean, clear filter on the mud of everyday challenges—helped me navigate both personal and professional obstacles. With her, I discovered that building your own brand means not only fostering a sense of community within your circle but also reaching beyond it. Her creation of Sister Circle stands as a testament to that belief—cultivating a community where genuine support and shared values thrive.

Even on days when I felt like I was dying inside, I learned to show up with a smile and honor my commitment to giving back. Stephanie practices what she preaches; she embodies authenticity and reliability, proving that while we're not meant for everyone, the people who truly understand and support you are meant to be part of your journey. Fostering genuine relationships—both personally and professionally—is essential for realizing our soul purpose and leaving a lasting legacy.

In the end, our lives are a tapestry of challenges and blessings. Despite the inevitable storms, the right people will walk with you through every season. With God as our foundation and genuine hearts leading the way, we can weather any storm and continue to shine—even when the path seems lonely.

Small Business Sister Story: Holly Lambrecht

Trusting the Nudge

In September 2022, I opened my own boutique online and out of my home. I had no idea what I was doing. I started my business to find other moms to share life with through our love of comfy, stylish clothing. In December, I saw Sister Circle and talked with Stephanie; I knew I needed to join. I went all in as a founding member. I came for the community and learned so much. I had a passion for people more than anything behind the scenes of business.

I pushed through 2023, but I wasn't making money—I was bleeding in the red month after month. A business I created for more freedom with my daughter and family started taking all my time. I began chasing money just to break even and pay off the debt. By December, I wanted out. I was mentally not okay and knew in my gut that if I didn't face the facts, things would never change.

Stephanie talked about trusting your intuition. At first, I doubted it—but I was *so* wrong. January 2024 came, and the heaviest thing I carried was my business. But in my head, quitting meant failure. I thought I just needed to push harder.

For the next five months, I was constantly anxious, forcing myself into my office to press shirts and fulfill orders—only to feel empty every time. The only place I found joy was in Sister Circle, surrounded by growth-minded women.

From January through May, I tried everything to increase sales and break even so I could walk away without burdening my family financially. I kept getting signs, nudges, and voices telling me it was okay. That I was meant for more. That closing my business wasn't a failure—it had served its purpose. It connected me with Stephanie and so many amazing women. It taught me about myself and led me to trust my gut.

In May, I closed my business. I typed my final announcement at least ten times before posting it. The second I hit "post," everything lifted. I no longer felt like I was carrying the weight of the world. Trusting my intuition lifted a massive burden from my life. I remember telling myself, *Something good is coming. Be patient and keep trusting.*

Just weeks later, Stephanie offered me a job with Sister Circle. I was in complete shock. My mind instantly said, *Me? How? I can't.* But my heart knew. This was my greater path. I adore people—knowing them, learning about and from them—and I knew Stephanie was who I wanted to learn from. Her guidance during my struggles, her light when I needed someone to listen—she is the true definition of a soul-preneur. She gave me the strength and courage to find my soul's purpose, and for that, I will always be grateful.

Part 4: Harvest Season

"I don't think each of us receives one harvest only— an after-death sort of payment for services rendered. I think we all get a lifetime full of little harvests—those small miracles that stand out from the rest of life, when we are one with nature, each other, and ourselves."

—Janene Wolsey Baadsgaard

Chapter 10:

End of an Era

My Bucket List Year

Have you ever asked, "Do I deserve this?" when life starts to get really good?

It was the beginning of my thirties, and I'd labeled it my "bucket list year." This year was all about doing the things I had been holding off on, couldn't afford, or couldn't get away from my business to do in my twenties and just making it happen!

Throughout the entire year, I continued to run my pop-up version of Zen and Pow, grew my real estate business and the clients I was serving, and experienced organic growth within the Sister Circle Membership. I was amazed as I watched my efforts and experience of entrepreneurship pay off in real estate and Sister Circle. It had taken me an entire decade to learn how to market, build and retain clients, sell, manage systems, and so much more. But now it allowed me to leap ahead in my first year of selling real estate and growing a small business community in ways I'd never imagined.

They say your first business isn't always the one that makes it, and I can see why that may be true. Usually, you start your first business out of pure passion with zero clue about how to run a business. It takes a lot of trial and error, effort, and learning the hard way to be able to make smart decisions. But even so, I wouldn't take any of it back because it made me who I am and taught me what I know to be true about business (and life).

By your second business, you already know what you wouldn't do again. For me, it solidified that I was meant to be doing something other than solely teaching yoga and fitness. I was meant to serve people on a deeper level, helping them build a lifestyle they love through real estate or small business ownership.

So, as my bucket list year went on, I continued to pour more into what *was* working in my businesses and having the best time of my life outside entrepreneurship. After years of choosing business first, I finally had a *life*. I wasn't teaching nearly as many classes, so I was able to finally prioritize my own health and wellness. I had more time on the weekends and weeknights to spend with friends and family, and I made having fun a priority, not a luxury.

I had made it through a full decade of planting, growing, and weathering storms in my small business ownership. And while I valued all these seasons greatly, this new chapter and season felt different.

I began to see how incredibly taxing it was on my mind, body, and soul to live in such a constant state of stress, fear, and worry. Even once we leave that state, it can take time for the mind and body to catch up with reality.

As my life started to improve in all areas after I made my big pivot, I started to feel myself questioning whether it was real, whether it was too good to be true, and whether I deserved to feel this good again.

Embracing your struggles when you are going through them can serve you greatly. But continuing to suffer, struggle, and be in a state of scarcity to feel like you deserve your success and happiness welcomes in the act of upper limiting.

If you haven't heard of upper limiting, it's the subconscious self-sabotaging that we do to ourselves when life begins to get really good. Whether it's a job promotion, a new great relationship, good health, or newfound abundance, we start to get a taste of the good life and question whether we deserve it. This is where the "I need to struggle to get success" mentality can get us hung up and twisted!

I found myself upper limiting myself a lot during my bucket list year. Let me give you an example of it. One day, I was headed out for a run through the quarry on top of the bluffs. This was not a bluff run like the one I describe earlier. In fact, it was a shorter, easier run with beautiful views and perfect seventy-degree weather. This run should have been a breeze compared to the other one. As we started out, I was thinking about how good life had been . . .

Then I started getting in my own head. Have you ever gotten in your own head, observed your thoughts, realized they were toxic, and then struggled to get out of your head? Well, that was me on this run. But this time, it wasn't about the run itself. I was questioning how my life had gotten so good and whether I deserved it. I started to create problems and pictures of the future that overwhelmed me.

I started to feel physically sick yet again. But this time, it wasn't from being hot or running up a bluff. It was my own mind playing tricks on me. I caught myself red-handed—upper limiting.

Then I started puking. But I didn't want to fall too far behind Ben and Yuka. So there I was, running and puking.

And I had another epiphany: This is what life feels like when we are doing things that scare the crap out of us, right? We have to keep running toward our goals and dreams. But sometimes, we're puking along the way. Hopefully, not actually. But maybe.

And then it hit me: Not only was life getting *really* good—like the way I wanted it to be and had been craving through years of suffering and struggling—but I felt like I was finally overcoming. Now I was ready to pursue some other big dreams and aspirations that made me feel sick to my stomach.

So I finished the run, knowing full well I'd sabotaged myself. There was nothing about that run that should have made me feel sick other than my own thoughts, fears, and limiting beliefs. But I was at least grateful for the self-awareness, and I knew it was a sign that I was on the right track toward big things.

And honestly, if your dreams don't make you sick in the slightest every once in a while, are you even challenging yourself? Are you even living up to your full potential? Are you even going for it?

How many of us struggle and suffer and make ourselves sick for nothing? For no big dreams. No crazy goals. No feat worth overcoming.

My mindset shifted during this bucket list year with my running epiphanies. As long as I'm alive, I'm going to keep moving—and moving in a direction that makes me at least a little nervous because that means I'm pursuing my full potential. But I vowed to catch myself when I found my mind upper limiting me and sabotaging me before I could reach my full potential.

When I caught myself upper limiting, I would step back from the task I was doing to check in with myself. I'd sit in my thoughts and get quiet, observing them. Oftentimes, we physically feel the yuck from upper limiting before we can fully notice the brain spiraling. So I'd feel that nervousness or pit in my stomach and ask myself, *What is causing this feeling? Why do I feel this way?* Once I called it out, I could usually talk myself out of feeling that way. Our brains *can* be rational.

How did I talk my way out of upper limiting? First, I asked myself, *Is this true? Or am I making up a story in my head that has not actually played out?* This was usually the case. Next, when I found fears running rampant and upper limiting my capacity for greatness, I did what I call "getting to the worst-case scenario" and decided if I could live with that or what my options would be if the worst thing actually happened. Now, I'm more of a best-case-scenario girl. But sometimes, it helped to consider the worst and see if I could live with it or play out what I would do.

For example, I told myself many times that if my business failed and I had no money, I could move back in with my loving parents, go get a teaching job with my degree, or serve and bartend. Did my first business "fail"? You could say so. But even so, none of the worst-case scenarios happened.

Then the final step was to remind myself of all the awful situations I had already survived and even come out better off——like my lawsuit, losing lots of money on build-outs, and ultimately leaving my brick-and-mortar studio. Drawing from past experience is one of my best strategies for talking myself out of anxiety, stress, and fears of what could be. So, whenever I found myself upper limiting, those steps got me back to living my best life.

In the bucket list year, I finally made my own happiness a priority and did things I never would have done before—like buying tickets to see Taylor Swift on The Eras Tour, signing up to go to Vegas to speak at an event, paddleboarding, enjoying beach days with friends, taking up gardening, reading more books for pure enjoyment, signing up for my own retreat and yoga experiences, and so much more.

One of the biggest bucket list items that Ben and I finally made a reality that year was going on our honeymoon! As I shared, we got married in 2020. And while we enjoyed our mini moon out west following our wedding, we really wanted to go somewhere tropical together. We envisioned lying on a beach, drinking piña coladas, and adventuring to new places in a different country. By the middle of that summer, I brought it up again. He agreed that it would be fun to go but still seemed far off. I was just coming out of the financial hole I had buried myself in. But I told him that if we made a plan and started saving, we could make it happen.

So we did. We picked Puerto Rico as our true honeymoon location, and we saved up the cash to make it a full one-week trip over our four-year wedding anniversary in November. The trip was quite an adventure, as we had no idea what we were planning and decided to stay half the time at an Airbnb in San Juan, then travel across the country to board a ferry to go to a private island called Vieques. We experienced two different scenes, from party life to quiet, small-town island life, but we had a blast. It was much-needed quality time together as we celebrated our anniversary and looked ahead to what was next for us.

This trip was all about being carefree and feeling like we were young again, without stress and worry. It was one of the first trips that allowed me to get away and truly, fully clock out and not worry about work—which was exactly what I needed. Our honeymoon meant a lot to us because we'd always talked about it being the last milestone we wanted to make sure happened before we wanted to try for a baby. But I knew there was another big shift coming and another hard decision that I had to make before the bucket list year ended and we could make starting our family a reality.

Growth Lessons

It is essential to work on your mindset as you grow your business so you can enjoy the success you deserve instead of thinking it always has to come through suffering and hard work. You have to know yourself well enough to stop your self-sabotage and recognize when you're upper limiting your success.

I wish I hadn't waited a full decade to start my bucket list year. Don't let your business or anything else stop you from checking off your own bucket list. Build a business that allows you to enjoy your life alongside it, even if it's checking off a few things a year that bring fun and spontaneity into your life. Don't wait until you accomplish x, y, and z in your business before you reward yourself for your hard work. You deserve to enjoy life *while* you're growing your business. Your bucket list can keep you from burning out.

More Than Building a Business

I spent my bucket list year deconstructing my entire life—pulling apart the pieces that no longer felt in alignment with who I am and where I was at while leaning into the pieces that still lit me up with my first business. What lit me up was and always had been the community I got to work out and do yoga with almost daily for ten years.

It was the early regulars who always made their way to my five a.m. class and kicked butt, no matter how tired they were.

The badass kickboxers I taught my MMA combos to who learned to love to punch and kick things hard, without fear!

My Wednesday evening chakra yogis who loved the spiritual side of yoga and had such soul-inspired conversations with me before and after class.

My Friday morning yogis who spent their mornings before work flowing with me, followed by a warm cup of butter pecan Cameron's coffee. (Don't forget the oatmeal cookie creamer!)

It was my barre class people who always came for some extra hip swings, dance moves, and "drop it lows," then left smiling and sweaty.

Even when members canceled over the years, many made it a point to come back every June for our outdoor anniversary DJ dance party, where we'd do the Thriller and my own made-up dance to my favorite song, "I Want to Dance with Somebody"!

I could go on and on over the memories I created while sweating, smiling, laughing, and crying with so many members, teammates, and friends. Our team and tribe held space for so many tough breakups, divorces, job changes, pregnancies, losses, COVID challenges, and so much more.

It was *always* about so much more than just fitness and yoga classes. We were known for creating community and positive experiences that eventually led people down a path to finding the highest version of themselves. While most people came for movement and weight loss, they found something so much deeper than the physical and the external.

I bet your business is about so much more than just the service and products you provide. It is always about the experience, how you make people feel, and the lasting, positive impact you create for your own tribe. I firmly believe you find your lifers and loyal clients when you focus more on the experience you cultivate and the personal relationships you build along the way. At the end of the day, people buy from people they like. So, if you want to build a business that stands out and can weather any storms, go the extra mile to be more than just a business. Instead, also be a smiling face, a safe space, and—even better—the creator of a community of people who can support each other along the way.

That is why I feel immense gratitude for each and every soul we had the privilege to positively impact along my decade-long journey of Zen and Pow. While I thought I was just chasing my dream studio, I came to realize that I was really opening the door for many people to find a more aligned version of themselves while I collected beautiful memories and experiences for the next chapter of my journey. (And along the way, I also found a more aligned version of myself.)

I needed to not just go through but grow through every hardship this business brought me and come out on the other side better because of it. It taught me resilience, persistence, passion, leadership, and all the business skills I needed to pivot and be successful in new industries and life experiences.

Whether you are scaling your first, second, or third business, or even if you decide not to pursue small business ownership forever, you are simply collecting along the way experiences, lessons, and memories that will serve you in your next chapter and evolution. I've come to see my first decade of business ownership not as a failure but as a journey I needed to embark on to get me to where I am today. And that has made all the difference. So, where has your business journey taken you and what has it taught you along the way?

Growth Lessons

Whether you realize it or not, you are building more than *just* a business. As a soul-preneur who has leaped into business ownership, be sure to showcase how you are unique and why you value your clients more deeply than just a transaction. Always go a little above the expectation to create meaningful experiences and memories. Ultimately, build relationships with your clients. Not only will they remember and appreciate it, but you will hold the memories as well.

Your efforts will never be for nothing if you take your memories, relationships, and experiences with you on your circle of growth. We're never really starting over. We are simply evolving with our experiences. The evolutions and chapters of your business are never in vain. They give you skills and experiences. And they teach you so much about what you do and don't want in life and in business. You're never starting over. You're ever evolving with your experiences and preparing for the next season of your small business journey. As I've said, you never know when something will come full circle.

Learning When to Let Go

Toward the end of my bucket list year, I was starting to feel overwhelmed and burned out again—a feeling I knew all too well at this point. Thankfully, it forced me to pause, pull myself out of the grind of running three businesses, get quiet, and ask for guidance. Burning myself out seemed to be a recurring theme for me over that last decade, and I knew I wanted to live life differently and build my businesses more sustainably than I had in the past. I was not going to let myself get burned out and reach a breaking point again.

I had just recently rebranded, renamed, and rebuilt Zen and Pow into Zen and Pow Soulciety, which was more than just fitness and yoga classes. It was a community of women who were coming together monthly and experiencing intentionally cultivated mind, body, and soul events and workshops. It was a genius idea to rebrand and rebuild my studio model to this because it was a unique concept. Not to mention, I loved creating all the fun experiences and events we did that summer, like paddleboarding, creating garden herb mixes, taking group hikes on my favorite trails, doing meditation classes, and so much more!

I was finally back to enjoying creativity and new experiences alongside amazing women each month like I had when I started this business! I thought this would fix the fact that I no longer felt passionate about what I had built Zen and Pow Studio to be and repair what wasn't working with that business. But I soon enough realized that it wasn't the business that was no longer working. I believe someone else could have taken what I had rebuilt into Zen and Pow Soulciety and run with it because it is what women desire and need—a community of wellness-focused women.

But it wasn't about fixing the business. I had come face-to-face with the fact that my passions had changed. It wasn't that the business needed fixing. Put simply, my dreams had evolved since my original vision. I'd spent the previous decade trying to scale a business, and I was no longer excited about rebuilding it over and over and over again.

One of the hardest lessons I have come to learn in business is that sometimes, things just aren't meant to work out for a reason. It doesn't mean you failed or could have fixed the problem. It's just that you evolve over time. Your dreams evolve too. So, as a big dreamer who's persistent and dedicated to seeing a goal through, I found it difficult to let this dream go.

Throughout that whole bucket list year, I was somehow able to balance three businesses while also pouring back into myself, my health, and my happiness. But as soon as I started to feel off, I knew something had to give. And I knew exactly what that was.

The dream I had spent an entire decade chasing was no longer for me. I had pivoted many times. I had rebuilt too many times to count. I had picked myself up from the deepest valleys this business had created for me. I had invested hundreds of thousands of dollars that I would never see again. I had gained and lost friendships that left deep wounds. I had built my entire life and identity around this business—and I don't regret a single moment of it.

I had to grow through everything this business threw at me, and all of it was for my own soul growth. It could never be in vain—especially if I used it for good and continued to share my story of struggles to inspire others to dig their way out of their darkest days.

At this point, though, I knew it was time. It was the last hard decision—knowing when to let go.

If I had made this decision the year prior, it would have felt too painful. I had too many wounds and scars that were too fresh. I couldn't have ended with things the way they were the year before. I needed the bucket list year to remind me of who I am and that I am more than the twenty-year-old yoga and fitness studio owner who chased her dream for an entire decade. I am proud of myself for doing the hard inner work that year while I slowly scaled back to heal, prioritize myself, and figure out what I really wanted.

So, on November 1, 2023, I made the last hard decision to let go of this business. I announced that I would be ending the era of Zen and Pow at the end of the year. For the first time in a long time, I felt complete *peace* around this decision. I had done a lot of healing since I had last decided to scale back and downsize, and I knew this was the right decision.

I walked inside Iron Works and up the stairs one more time, recalling how I ran up and down those stairs many times a day for so many years—from the beginning of my business journey to the last year of scaling back. I reflected on the room and looked around before setting up my mat to teach my last class of the decade.

Well, there we were—a whole decade after it had all started. It was right before Christmas, so I was excited to teach my usual holiday HIIT full of my favorite holiday remixes, Santa squats, jingle bell burpees, and the rest of my creative exercises.

The tribe brought their A game. We worked hard, and I saw so many smiles throughout class. We started stretching and cooling down, and I couldn't help but feel the bittersweetness of the moment. I felt immense gratitude for all the people in the room that day who'd stuck with me through all the highs and lows. And I also felt sadness for the ending of an era—not only in my business but in my life. I knew that going into the new year was going to feel radically different without these people, my weekly classes, and Zen and Pow Studio as part of my weekly routine.

I said, "Take a big inhale up and exhale a positive thought . . ." which was my usual closing. "Thank you all for coming to sweat with me today. I hope you know how much I appreciate you all!" That was about all I could muster without letting too many tears fall. My eyes were misty, as were many in the room that day.

I hugged everyone, said my goodbyes, and locked up that room one last time. *Deep breath, Steph.* Many days felt like years, but the years passed by in the blink of an eye. The days are long, but the years are short—and the memories and friendships made will last a lifetime.

Zen and Pow was my first baby. If you've created something from the beginning—like a business—you know exactly what I mean. I birthed, grew, nurtured, and loved it so dearly. But I was in a new season of life, and I was ready to start my family and birth my own baby. While I trusted the timing of everything, I had already waited what felt like *years* to start my family while I watched many friends and family around me start to have babies. I wanted that too. But I knew that dream would never be attainable if I wasn't willing to let go of my first child.

I surrendered to my intuition, once again, and closed the doors on that first business at the end of my thirty-first trip around the sun. It was the end of an amazing era. But with that always comes the birth of a new one.

Growth Lessons

As you grow your business, allow your business to evolve and grow with you and your dreams too! Evolution is part of the growth circle, and with that comes letting go of goals and dreams that no longer serve you in the new seasons of your life and business. This is a huge part of the small business journey that I wish more people would share because it always feels like failure when you're going through it. But it's just a natural evolution. What you built was not for nothing. All along, you were building much more than just a business, and every experience brought you the skills, relationships, and opportunities you needed to succeed in your next season.

Trust yourself and your gut to know when it's time to let go of something. The signs will usually be there. You just have to trust the timing and have the courage to make the hard decision. Letting go is never easy. But every time you let go of something that is not serving you, you open up the doors for the next opportunity to find you.

Chapter Reflections

Reflection Questions:

❖ Can you recall an experience when life got really good and you began to upper limit yourself and question whether you deserved it? Or did you wonder when the next bad thing was going to happen?

❖ What would be on your bucket list for this year? How can you commit to making it happen?

❖ How are you building more than just a business? What lessons, relationships, and experiences have you gained through your small business journey?

❖ Think back to a time when you had to embrace a change. How did you know it was the right decision to allow yourself to evolve?

❖ Are you holding onto something that is no longer serving you in your life or business? What is stopping you from letting go?

Intentional Action:

• New Small Business Owner: So much of how you experience your small business journey comes down to one thing—your mindset. How you choose to perceive your challenges, your circumstances, and your evolution is up to you. Grab a piece of paper and write down all the skills, experiences, and connections you gathered from your experiences before your business. This is probably a great resume! Refer to this list when you feel unprepared for or overwhelmed by being a beginner in business. You already have skills, experiences, and connections from your life before your business. *Use them.* Continue to work on your mindset as you grow in your journey, learn to catch yourself when you are upper limiting, and find what helps you tune back into what you desire and your innate ability to co-create it for your life.

- Seasoned Small Business Owner: My guess is that you've sacrificed a lot of your personal life at this point in your business. So, make a bucket list. Not for life, though. Make it for this *year.* No matter where you are in your business, figure out how you can make it happen because you deserve to reward yourself after years of putting your business first. If you are feeling the desire to make some changes in your business, take some time to figure out how you are holding yourself back from what is no longer serving you. What would it look like to let go of it and evolve? Write down what you would do if you could let go of the part of your life or business that is no longer working. I bet you'd probably be able to get to your bucket list *more.* You can do this, and you deserve it. Catch yourself upper limiting and allow yourself to expand and evolve alongside your dreams!

Ben and I on our 3 year anniversary honeymoon
in Puerto Rico (2023)

Chapter 11:

In My Mom Era

Creating Space for the Next Thing

I'm a New Year's junkie. I love the feeling of a fresh start, new goals, and dreams. I guess that's the visionary in me. For the past few years, Ben and I have had a tradition of making a vision board together on New Year's Eve. It has become one of my favorite things to do around the holidays!

For the last few years, whatever I put on my side of the vision board still felt far away. Things like meeting business goals, hitting health goals, buying a new vehicle, and building my savings account back up. Over the past decade, my business goals never quite came to fruition how I thought they would. Then I went through a two-year period of transitioning everything.

But 2024 felt different.

I had finally made the hard decision to let go of my first business and move forward into the new year with new energy and a new weekly schedule. And for the first time in so long, I had *space* again. Not just space in my schedule but space in my mind, body, and soul. Space to dream again and space to create exciting new beginnings.

And I knew exactly what I wanted to fill that space with.

Ben and I printed out for the vision board pictures of what we desired, and I started to fill up my side of the vision board with photos of pregnancy. I wrote a due date of October 2024 to add to our family, alongside goals, like decluttering the whole house, designing the nursery, having a healthy pregnancy, buying a new vehicle, and a few other personal goals—like finishing this book!

We'd made it through the last milestone we needed to hit—going on our honeymoon—before starting our family, so this was the year. And I could feel it . . .

I couldn't wait to get a positive pregnancy test and experience the excitement of a *new* dream coming true for me—one I had waited so long to step into.

The end of January came around, and I couldn't wait to take a pregnancy test. But my heart sank when I got my period. Still, I kept receiving signs telling me to surrender, get back in the flow of fun, and enjoy this new phase of my life. I knew that the baby would come when they were ready. I trusted that and surrendered the outcome for the next month.

I started taking up new hobbies for myself, like dancing! I couldn't wait to try adult dance classes at my friend Michelle's local studio, I&E. I even signed up for a self-love retreat around Valentine's Day. I knew I needed to learn to love myself again before I ever became a mother.

At the retreat, we made a vision board. I thought, *What the heck. Why not make another one?* So I filled it with words and phrases like, "Restore your inner glow," "Magic," "Shifting," "Renew your sense of purpose," "Go with the flow," and "Manage life's transitions." This board became my reminder to stay open, relaxed, and free. I even had a tarot card reading at the retreat that ended with The Mother card. It felt like such a positive sign for my pregnancy journey!

I was tempted to take an early pregnancy test that month, but I didn't want to end up disappointed like the month before. So I stayed patient and open and continued to pour into myself and find joy in the journey.

When the last week of the month came, my period was late. I finally caved and took a test, but the positive sign was very faint. I didn't believe it and thought I'd wait another day. Another day passed, and it was another faint positive. I was still in shock. I thought, *I'll wait one more day* . . .

Friday finally came, and I knew it would be the day. I could feel it. I woke up early, before Ben did, to use the bathroom. And sure enough, it was a very clear and bold *positive*. I couldn't believe it! I wanted to surprise him, so I hid the test and slid back into bed, waiting for him to get up and get in the shower. While he was in the shower, I put a cute little bandana on Yuka that said, BIG SIS.

When he came out of the shower and into the bedroom to get dressed, I was sitting up in bed.

"What is Yuka wearing?" he asked.

"Why don't you read it?" I responded.

"Just tell me what it says."

My eyes rolled back, and I asked, "Are you serious? Why don't you just read it?"

He clearly was not getting it and was ruining my surprise. Finally, he read the bandana and looked at me with big eyes. "You're pregnant?" he asked.

When I nodded, he exclaimed, "Congrats!" and gave me a hug.

And that is how my mom era began.

Now I had this big secret to keep, at least for a little bit. But I was overjoyed to learn our due date was October 29. For the first time in a long time, my life was falling into place how I had hoped—and right on time. This baby felt like a miracle I had long awaited, and I promised myself that I would continue to do all the things I wanted to do that year so I could take them along with me. I wanted to build so many beautiful memories of pregnancy with this little miracle inside my belly . . . So that's what I did while growing this baby.

They were a part of my annual Sister Circle Summit, jumping around with me on stage.

They were there when Ben and I went to see Greta Van Fleet in concert and made our way up to Michigan for a family camping trip in the Upper Peninsula.

They were there as I attended many business conferences, from Minneapolis to Arizona, where I went on a solo trip to the PowerHouse Women event at twenty-eight weeks.

They were there through every workout, walk, and dance class as I stayed committed to my health every single week.

They were there as I danced my way through the year, performing in contemporary company and hip-hop at the outdoor dance concert at thirty weeks.

They were there through listings, showings, closings, Sister Circle meetings, and everything in between.

I never want this baby to be the reason I stop doing the things I love that light me up. I want this child to be the reason I follow my dreams. Because they will always be watching me.

The next opportunity, person, or experience often can't find us until we let go of what's not serving us to make space for what *will* serve us in the next chapter. Where in your life are you blocking that next thing from finding you because you're holding onto old dreams, relationships, and experiences that are no longer serving you? Do you have a new dream? A new vision to pursue?

Growth Lessons

When one door closes, another one always opens. But we have to close the first door! What are you holding onto that is keeping your next door from opening? Allow yourself to create space for the next thing and find joy in the journey of surrendering. I believe that the more we can be intentional about what we want (like with a vision board) while actively working toward it, the closer we come to experiencing it. The hardest part is surrendering when and how it comes to us. But through intention, action, and surrendering, you will, soon enough, watch your new visions come to life before your eyes.

Trust the Timing and Surrender

As the year went on, I couldn't wait to find out if it was a boy or a girl. I always had the vision that I'd be a boy mom because I come from a family of many girls. I just thought that wouldn't happen for me.

If you know me, you know I love throwing parties and celebrating all the things. So, of course we had to throw a gender reveal party that was full of my favorite pregnancy cravings. Everyone wore either pink or blue to indicate what they thought the gender would be. I had my dear friend Kelly fill a punching bag piñata with appropriately colored items, as she was the only person who knew the gender based on our ultrasound.

Ben and I were both dead set on it being a boy. In fact, when we went in for our twenty-week ultrasound two days before the party, we told the technician that we didn't want to know the gender. Instead, we had her write it down on a piece of paper.

"The baby is really moving around," she said as we were in our appointment. I looked at Ben with a little panic on my face because I'd planned this party for two days later.

"Are you going to be able to tell if it's a boy or a girl? We have a gender reveal party planned for Friday . . ." I said nervously.

"Oh yes. I saw what I needed to see already," she stated very matter-of-factly.

Well, that just confirmed what we thought: *It's a boy*. Why else would she say that she'd seen what she needed to see? So we left that night with 99.9 percent assurance that our instincts were correct!

Friday came around, Kelly filled the piñata, and our yard was full of our best friends and family members who were ready for the big reveal showdown. (Of course it was a fight night theme.)

Ben let me punch first, but I knew I wouldn't make much of a dent in it. Besides, I wanted him to break it open to reveal the surprise. On his first punch, the piñata swung and just skimmed the top of my head! Watching the video in slow motion still cracks me up to this day. He just about took me out with that punch. I held the plant hanger it was tied to so he could take another swing, and I saw what looked like pink confetti on the ground. But I didn't say anything.

Then he threw a big left hook and cracked it right open. This might be the one time my intuition was wrong in the last decade. Pink confetti and pink items flew out, then everyone screamed, "It's a *girl!*" Ben threw his hands up to face in shock, and I was laughing so hard. I gave him a big hug. We were both in shock.

I'm going to be a girl mom, I thought. *Wow.* It took some time for that to set in. As I've shared, I'd never pictured it before. I'd always pictured myself with boys. So my entire perspective started to change. Then I realized how many fun things we would get to do together, and I got even more excited for this little baby.

As the rest of the summer carried on, I carried her with so much love and joy inside me, and I watched many of the other visions and dreams I'd set for the year come to fruition as I continued to surrender to this new chapter and trusted the timing of dreams manifesting.

While I had entered my "mom van era" the previous year out of necessity, this year, I entered it out of choice. I had wanted to buy a new vehicle in my bucket list year, but I didn't want to take out another loan. So I'd decided I would buy a new vehicle *only* if I could pay cash for it. I held off and grew in patience as I drove my mom's old "trusty, rusty" Dodge Caravan for another year. It got the job done. And, believe it or not, it was an upgrade from my previous vehicle.

I have quite the history of unfortunate car luck—from my engine overheating to a tire flying off, to needing to pour water to cool my radiator, to no radio or AC because I didn't have the money to buy a new one in the previous decade. While I was embarrassed to drive the mom van at first, I fell in love with vans and all the space they provide. Plus, I just needed something to get me around town to teach classes, attend appointments, get to showings, and make meetings. So, thanks for letting me borrow the van, Mom and Dad!

As the year went on, I finally had enough to buy a new vehicle. But, dang, I had worked so hard for that cash that I just kept driving the van. I didn't care about the comments or what people probably thought because I had a goal, and that's all that mattered. I was patient about finding the right new vehicle for me. And once I found out I was having a baby, the idea of the mom van became even more practical. It was my vehicle of choice, thanks to all the space it would give our family.

Ben and I were just about to take our summer trip up to Ironwood, Michigan, in July. It was our last camping trip for just us and Yuka before the baby. But we still didn't have a reliable vehicle for the five-hour drive. So, a few weeks before the trip, I started looking. I thought, *Wouldn't it be nice if I could find a reasonably priced vehicle before our trip so we could enjoy it even more?* So I called my dad, who grew up working and owning a car lot, and we started the search.

In a matter of a few days, we found a three-year-old silver Dodge Pacifica that was shiny, beautiful, just down the road from my house, and available for an amazing price. I ended up spending less than I'd even anticipated, and it was practically brand-new! We test-drove it, and I knew it was the one. So I made the purchase just days before we headed up north for our last family road trip for three in our brand-new Pacifica, which was as comfy as could be.

As you know now from reading my story, this purchase would not have been possible just two years earlier, when I had only pennies to my name. I was digging my way out of debt and was so ashamed because I'd never thought I would be in that financial position in the first place.

But it taught me so many lessons that I'll never forget. It also showed me what's possible when you put your best foot forward, no matter your past, and focus on your future. Drive that trusty, rusty van so you can pay cash for the vehicle you really want! Who cares what others think? You have your goals and know where you're going. Stay patient, be persistent, and keep moving through the hard times. So, after years of putting a new vehicle on my vision board, I *finally* got to cross off that goal and feel such immense pride and appreciation for it.

We often try to micromanage and control the timing of our lives. But when we just trust and surrender to it, we often realize there was a plan all along—and it's better than we could have even imagined. Faith, trust, and surrender have been a huge part of my entrepreneurship journey. They have allowed my dreams and visions to expand to be far greater than anything I could do on my own.

Growth Lessons

Entrepreneurship requires so much patience. You don't get to reap the reward the day you plant the seed. My patience and persistence paid off in waiting to purchase the right vehicle at the right time. It would have been easy to just go buy a brand-new vehicle and take out another loan to add to my monthly debts—especially in the name of not wanting people to judge me for the rusty van I was driving. Small business owners make many sacrifices to build a dream. And that often comes at the price of letting go of what others think and staying focused on our goals and vision for the future. We have to be able to see what's possible when it's not right in front of us, which comes from having faith.

Soul-preneurship requires an immense amount of faith, trust, and surrender. It's so important to believe in a higher power that you can surrender to whenever you need faith and guidance. Learning to let go of what you think your perfect plan is for your business and life allows you to open up to opportunities and possibilities far better than anything you could have imagined for yourself or accomplished on your own.

Intentional Entrepreneurship

As summer turned to fall, my baby grew from a little bump to the size of a squash by October. The realness of her arrival started to finally set in. I spent all spring and summer preparing, from setting up my businesses for maternity leave to decluttering the entire house and preparing the nursery.

I was adamant about having a real, true, paid, and mostly checked-out three-month maternity leave. I had spent the previous decade grinding and hustling so hard in my businesses, sacrificing a lot of time with family and friends, and ultimately delaying the beginning of my own family. *No* more. I owed it to myself to create a maternity leave and show other female entrepreneurs that it is possible to take time out of your business if you're willing to put in the intentional effort and work.

I knew it would take months to prepare for. But, once again, I was up for the challenge! I hired part-time support for Small Business Sister Circle, prepared my real estate clients to be supported by my team, trained eleven new Sister Circle certified coaches to take over all meetings, and started planning for 2025 in the summer of 2024 so I could work ahead and not feel rushed coming back from maternity leave in the new year. I thought of every possible piece of my businesses and how I could delegate, outsource, or work ahead so I could soak up as many baby snuggles as possible without feeling pulled back into my work.

I knew I didn't want to be stressed going into labor or once I was holding a newborn. I was in my full-on mom era, and I have to say, I am so proud of this version of myself for prioritizing myself, my baby, and my family instead of my work for the first time in my adult life. It's hard to do when you're a creative, passionate entrepreneur, but I prepared myself so much for this season that I was ready to reap the rewards.

I coined the term *intentional entrepreneurship* from my own personal effort to prioritize my life ahead of my business because I had spent way too long doing the opposite. I spent my entire twenties fitting my personal life around my business. Intentional entrepreneurship is about the opposite—creating a profitable, sustainable, and scalable business that would allow me the freedom to enjoy my life alongside it.

Let's break these down because what took me over a decade to figure out could save you so much time, effort, and money!

Profitability is important. If you don't have any profit, you have a very expensive hobby. We all have expensive hobbies at some point or another, but it can't be forever! It is super common to not have profitability right away in your business. It could even be years. But you have to have a plan for profitability and a system to get there. This is where you go back to the earlier lessons I shared about getting gritty, starting small, and using your resources until you can get out of the red and into the green.

You have to decide how long you're willing to pour time, effort, and energy into a dream that isn't paying you back in money. For me, it was easy to scrape by in my twenties. I was used to being broke and had no family to provide for. But, as I had gotten married, had bought a house, and wanted to start a family, the business not being profitable was no longer an option.

Sustainability is an important consideration. It's also where I see so many small business owners burning themselves out over and over and over again. Are you building a business that allows you to step away from it and work *on* the business instead of in it? Can you take time away to enjoy life alongside business? So many small business owners are running at a pace that only leads to burnout and loss of passion for what they're doing. I've experienced this soul-level burnout many times in my own journey!

Simplify your systems and processes, then build a team of support to help you scale your business sustainably over time, whether that is bringing on interns, hiring a team of part-time employees, getting freelance help, or delegating. You cannot be the only person doing all the things without time to recoup your energy.

Just as important as sustainability is scalability. So often, we think bigger and more are always better. Often, we scale our business at the cost of profitability. Or maybe we scale our business at the cost of sustainability. More often than not, we scale at the cost of both sustainability *and* profitability.

And that is a fast track to burnout and feeling like a failure.

I did this.

I used to think the bigger studio I had, the more money I would make. It was the opposite. I was paying more overhead to staff more classes. And with help on the back end, the profit continued to shrink with every big leap and studio expansion I made. What I assumed would catapult me forward by taking a big leap of faith actually sent me backward financially.

And I continued to grow my team, clients, and offerings, only to realize that scaling is one of the hardest things to do as a soul-preneur. Growth creates growing pains, and you'll be forced to weather seasons you never thought you'd face. As soon as I started to scale, I hit most of my hardest seasons as a small business owner. That's not to say you shouldn't scale. Just do so in a way that is sustainable *and* profitable. That is the absolute *key*!

As I've said many times, my decisions were all part of my path, and I don't take any of it back. But when I finally figured all of this out, I realized that my first business was not profitable, sustainable, *or* scalable. And I was chasing it at the cost of my entire lifestyle.

It hit me hard when I realized that what I had built would never allow me to be pregnant, have a baby, and grow a family without sacrificing my financial, physical, and mental health. This realization was one of my biggest reasons for pivoting, re-envisioning, and letting go of my first baby.

No more. It was time to redefine my idea of success, which was to build businesses to be profitable, sustainable, and scalable so I could enjoy the freedom that entrepreneurship offers alongside my business and reap the rewards of my hard work in my harvest season. And it became my mission to help other female small business owners realize this a lot sooner than I did.

Because I made the hard decisions to let go and let in new dreams and visions, I was in such a better place and able to enjoy my pregnancy. *This* was my harvest season, and it just happened to fall in the middle of fall. I could feel all my dreams and visions aligning perfectly as I settled into maternity leave with peace, joy, and gratitude. I created this season for myself by not just being intentional in the years prior but by allowing for a season of surrender—surrendering to God and the plan he had for me all along that I just couldn't see.

When I was walking through my deepest and darkest valley, feeling like a failure, and walking away from a dream and identity that I thought defined me, I couldn't see this season. I couldn't imagine what was possible. Everything felt so uncertain and foreign because I hadn't been in a place of stability for so long. I would've never pictured myself on a three-month maternity leave, soaking up moments with my newborn baby. I couldn't see how much good was in store for me when I was in the thick of it.

But there were always signs that I was on the right path. Being the soul-preneur I am, I have always been fascinated by the idea of past lives and fully believe that we are souls on a journey, learning the lessons we need for growth and our purpose in human form. I regularly received reiki energy healing from my friend, Shannon, a couple of times a year, and when I learned she was offering past-life readings, I knew it was just what I needed to gain some clarity on my path and why I was facing so many challenges.

This six-hour session was one of the most fascinating experiences I've ever had! If you've never experienced this for yourself, you spend some time initially figuring out what you want to know and ask your higher self, guides, or past lives. Then whoever is guiding your session, which in this case was Shannon, took me into a deep state of relaxed hypnosis. From there she simply asked questions to gain the clarity I was seeking. The best part is it's all recorded, so I've been able to play back the recording many times since that session, and every time I do I learn new things and have insane *aha* moments that have come to fruition!

In playing back my session, I heard my higher self say, "She knows the struggle and the pain that she's gone through. And as long as she can turn it into something positive, helpful, and good, it will be the thing that actually gets her to where she wants to go."

Shannon replied, "So she needs to reflect on all the things that have created challenges for her and turn it into something useful? And will she be able to help a lot of people this way?"

"More than she even realizes," I heard my voice say. By the way, it is strange to hear yourself talking about yourself in the third person. That alone was proof to me to believe this was my higher self talking.

"Good," said Shannon, "she needs to know that her efforts will be fruitful in helping others."

To my astonishment I replied, "It's like she planted seeds in her past life. Just like a farmer would. And in this life, she can reap some of those rewards and actually experience some of the harvest."

It turned out in my most recent past life I was a farmer that worked myself to death. I felt like a failure because I never experienced the rewards of my hard work. I never got to experience my harvest season in that life. Gaining this insight that I got to start over in this life planting new seeds, growing, and albeit weathering many storms still, I now get to experience the fruits in helping others. I learned through my past life session that my first business was just a steppingstone to my higher purpose; it was my education in the school of hard knocks and what gives me credibility to help other business owners along their own journey.

All along, I trusted the path, my soul, and the growth I needed to evolve. And it took me to exactly where I was meant to be—happy, peaceful, and free. Free to create the life I desire with intentionality.

That's the funny thing about life and God's plan: You can see it only when you look backward. Remember, hindsight is 20/20. If only we could trust the destruction to lead us exactly to the rebirth we need to experience. If only we could believe there is more in store for us—visions and dreams that are unrealized, unimagined, and better than we ever thought possible when in the middle of a deep valley. If only we could surrender to the lessons we are meant to learn and the soul growth we were sent here to experience so we could know there is a season of harvest waiting for us if we are willing to plant new seeds and start again.

Growth Lessons

Be intentional about your business from the beginning so you can strategically build a business that is profitable, sustainable, and scalable—and avoid burnout along the way. Avoid growth for the sake of growth and grow in a way that is sustainable and scalable over time so you don't need to sacrifice your health or well-being. Always know your numbers and have a plan for profitability so you feel rewarded by your business sooner rather than later. While many businesses may take years to be profitable, make sure you are happy with your decisions to continue to invest in your dream so you don't grow to resent your business.

The best part about soul-preneurship is that you get to define what success looks like for you in life and in business. There is no linear path or cookie-cutter way to find success. So, be sure to get intentional in your entrepreneurship journey so you can build a business that fits into your life—not the other way around.

Chapter Reflections

Reflection Questions:

❖ Can you think of an experience where you let go of something and the next right person or opportunity came your way?

❖ Do you have a new dream or vision you would like to pursue?

❖ Have you yet to experience the rewards of your hard work? How can you surrender your outcome and trust the timing of your path?

❖ Is your business profitable, sustainable, and scalable? If not, how can you get intentional with all three to find more freedom from your business?

❖ Define your version of success in your business and your life. What would that look and *feel* like?

Intentional Action:

• New Small Business Owner: If you haven't already, I highly recommend creating a vision board for your business that focuses more on your desired feelings than how it looks on the outside. Get intentional about your business from the beginning so you can avoid building something that is unprofitable, unscalable, and unsustainable. Trust me, future you will thank you! Write down what your definition of success is in business and in life, then post it somewhere you'll see it. Update it every year to allow that definition to change and evolve as you do. The more intentional you are about building your business to support your lifestyle from the beginning, the smarter your decisions will be along the way. And grow in patience for your harvest season—and stay open. It rarely comes to us how we think it will.

- Seasoned Small Business Owner: At this point, you've probably experienced some seasons of harvest or had glimmers of it along your journey. Maybe you don't feel fully satisfied, though. If you don't, maybe it's time to update your definition of success. You can take the same advice I give the new small business owner above. My challenge to you as a seasoned small business owner is this: Can your business run without *you*? If not, that is worth getting intentional about. Even if you don't want to scale, how can you get it sustainable and profitable *without you*? Work on that. If you're not sure, reach out to me. I'd love to help!

Small Business Sister Story: Maryann Baldwin

Seeds of Integrity: How a Lifetime of Showing Up Led to an Unimaginable Harvest

One of my biggest life values is integrity. For me, integrity means following through on your commitments, showing up for others and for yourself, when *and* how you say you will. That sounds so simple and obvious, but following a thirty-five-year career in corporate environments, you'd be surprised how often people don't show up on time or show up prepared for whatever was planned!

The best part of showing up is that life isn't always predictable. Because you were there and someone else wasn't, you just might learn about a new opportunity before everyone else! Just by showing up, you can realize a harvest that sets you apart from others more often than you would think.

And that was it. Throughout my career, I just kept showing up, prepared for the task or opportunity at hand. Once others noticed that reliability, more opportunities came my way, creating a path that I never could have plotted out on my own. I sowed a lot of seeds this way, and many grew in ways I'd never imagined, like starting a business in what most people would call retirement.

My career harvest was a bountiful one. When I decided to get off the corporate rollercoaster and "retire," I had a deep desire to give back in gratitude for all life had provided to me. Retirement in my mind represented the period in my life when I could truly get serious about giving back. What I never imagined was that that would be through entrepreneurship!

My original desire was to help others discover ways they could take charge of their fitness and wellness through the opportunity to purchase a gym and lead others through fitness classes and personal training—where I first connected with Stephanie at a Pilates training! It was a wonderfully gratifying role, and the entrepreneurship piece was icing on the cake. But I knew I was ready to create space for something new . . .

The role of fitness coaching, learning how to manage a small business, and my lifelong roles in corporate marketing, along with my own intuition, led me to my next chapter of entrepreneurship. I sold my gym and opened up a coworking space in my small town of Lansing, Iowa, to serve as a business coach and counselor.

There is great gratification in learning about someone's spark of an idea for a product or service or business and walking side-by-side with them to bring that spark to life. Entrepreneurship can be a lonely path, so being that person who "gets you" and can help you overcome barriers to achieve your vision alongside creating a space to connect is a role I feel I was born to play at this season of my life. I feel so grateful to be able to intentionally spend my retirement giving back with such purpose!

Shortly after I opened The Works co-working space, I reconnected with Stephanie just as she was launching the Sister Circle membership. Two past gym owners turned business coaches seeking to create community and opportunities for connection. A perfect example of connections coming full circle and how you just never fully know what lies ahead.

But by simply showing up, being prepared for what you do know, and trusting that the effort you make today will most certainly lead to a bountiful harvest in the future, the journey is so much more enjoyable.

Dancing on stage with 90+ attendees at
Sister Circle Summit (2024)

Chapter 12:

Reaping the Rewards of the Harvest Season

It was October 29 and the perfect day to write this last chapter. It was officially baby girl's due date, and I was feeling extra reflective. We were blessed with an abnormally warm day. Eighty degrees at the end of October in Wisconsin is quite rare. I embraced the warmth, knowing it could very well be our last warm day of 2024.

It was actually the last of many things, and I began to feel a tear forming at the bittersweet realization that life as I knew it was about to end as our next chapter began . . .

It could be my last morning waking up and looking down at my pumpkin-sized belly, which was carrying my baby safely and soundly within me.

It could be my last good night of good sleep for months. I was hoping not, but I was also being realistic.

It could be my last morning waking up without having to take care of anyone but me.

It could be my last night as just Stephanie before I took on the role of mom forever—which was hard to believe.

It could be my last morning of just Ben, Yuka, and me sipping coffee quietly together before the sun rose.

It could also be my last morning walk with Yuka on our usual route around the neighborhood before the winter season. So I figured I better get outside and enjoy it.

I got Yuka harnessed up. She was ready to rock, per usual, as she loved this part of her morning routine. The day was so warm that I needed just my yoga pants, tank top, and slip-on sandals. I threw my headphones on, as I always listen to podcasts or music on walks. Then we headed out the door.

Not a minute in, my headphones stopped playing music. I thought that was strange. I tried to reconnect the Bluetooth, but nothing was coming out. So I took it as a sign to get quiet and listen. I slid the headphones down around my neck and decided to just listen to the sounds of nature around me instead on this beautiful morning walk.

It's amazing how much more observant we are when we're not listening to anything. I witnessed probably hundreds of leaves falling down, making their descent from the trees, effortlessly. I listened to the wind rustling through the leaves, gently swaying branches until leaves flowed from them with ease. All the colors of fall—red, orange, yellow, and brown leaves—floated to the ground, just as natural as could be.

Fall is my favorite season, and while I observed the beauty all around me, I couldn't help but feel immense gratitude as I realized that this was my harvest season. Oftentimes, we are so focused on the future that we forget to be grateful for the present moment. And your present moment might just be the thing you prayed for in seasons of planting, growing, and weathering the storms. If you don't stop to soak it up, you might just miss it.

And with that, you'll miss the whole point of the changing of the seasons and the ever-evolving journey you've been on. The highs and the lows you've endured were all part of your circle of growth. Your path to your purpose is full of pivots, twists, turns, valleys, and mountaintops.

As I felt very present on this walk with Yuka, I couldn't help but think of my own seasons of planting, growing, and weathering the storms that had led me to the harvest season of enjoying my maternity leave after over a decade of hustling hard. I was soaking up the sweetest moments before the arrival of the baby I'd prayed for— the baby whose existence wouldn't have been possible if I hadn't endured my darkest, hardest seasons.

This simple walk on our usual path on an ordinary Tuesday was anything but ordinary as I realized how full circle life can be—and how we must cherish every season of the cycles and trust in our path. It's always leading us to exactly where we're meant to be.

I realized that over the last decade of my life, I'd simply been growing through what I was going through. And, once again, I realized that small business ownership is a lot like gardening: planting seeds, enduring growing seasons, and weathering storms, cycles, and seasons, all to hopefully experience the harvest season, eventually. We have to grow through all the highs and lows to fully appreciate the harvest.

Planting

In my planting season, I learned to embrace my small-town Midwest roots and followed my own path into entrepreneurship. I did this despite feeling a bit misunderstood or like I didn't quite fit in with those around me. Because I felt like I didn't fit in, I took the leap to create my own community and launch my very first baby, Zen and Pow Studio, at the age of twenty.

This business was a huge turning point in my life that opened up so many doors for planting seeds of dreams for my future. But I had to learn to start small while still dreaming big, which meant getting gritty to get started and allowing myself room to grow into my goals. Without the courage to launch my first business, I never would have stumbled into MMA, where I faced so many fears and failures by putting myself out there. Through MMA, I planted the seeds for the mental resilience and ability to power through hard seasons of business when it would have been easier to quit. Little did I know that this mindset would become my fighter mentality for my soon-to-come seasons of growing pains and introduce me to my soon-to-be husband.

What seeds do you wish to plant for your business or life? How can you get started today? You won't grow what you don't intentionally plant.

Growing

You don't reap your rewards the day you plant the seed. You must grow patience for the growing season. I needed seasons of growth to propel me into my next levels, which only got harder and more challenging. But through trusting my gut to take big leaps and avoid red flags, I still had to learn many lessons the hard way. I knew soul-preneurship would come with hard lessons and lots of hustle, which made it challenging to balance life and business. I spent years watering my seeds by working hard—often to the point of burnout. I finally found the right mentor and space for my business, and I weeded through many difficult challenges and growing pains.

Where do you need to practice patience for yourself and your business in your growing season? What does watering, weeding, and waiting look like for you?

Weathering Storms

The weather, seasons, and cycles of gardening are just as unpredictable as business and life! There are always going to be storms outside your control, and that's when quickly jumping into action to lead with your values will serve you well—even when it means going against the grain.

You can control only yourself, which is why it's so important to continue to search for glimmers of sunlight among your dark days and most destructive storms. You realize through these storms that some people are a season for a reason, while others stick it out with you to celebrate the sunny days. Create the community of people you need for the season you're in. You'll likely experience seasons of drought in which you may hit financial hardships that require you to evolve, pivot, and re-envision your life and business in a more sustainable way. Just don't let the storms stop you from enjoying the process, reflecting on how far you've come, and continuing to dream of a bright future.

It's important to recognize the cycles and seasons of small business ownership. Sometimes you're up, and other times you're down. How can you take it all in stride, focus on what's inside your circle of control, and continue to hold hope for the harvest?

Harvest

Soon enough, you'll have an *aha* moment, like my walk with Yuka. That's when you'll know you've made it to your harvest season! You'll finally learn to accept the harvest without second-guessing your worth because you gained the experience you needed, healed, and worked on your mindset. So you can now let go and create space for your next seeds to be planted.

But before you plant new seeds for your next season, be sure to soak up and enjoy the harvest from your garden and fully appreciate all the growth and storms you weathered to get to it. You can look back at the full circle and see how trusting yourself, following your path, and surrendering your vision allowed you to step into your harvest season.

You can't experience the harvest without the planting and growth seasons, which often take years of being patient and weathering the storms. But you can eventually fully appreciate and celebrate the harvest season of things working out in your favor. Allow yourself to grow through all your seasons of planting, drought, replanting, and surrendering so you can fully appreciate your own harvest season in life and in business.

Enjoying the Harvest Season

Yuka and I finished up our walk, and I snapped a picture of us outside our yard. I wanted to cherish this day and soak up this full-circle moment. Then I sat down to type this last chapter and celebrate by taking the rest of the day off—just as I imagined my maternity leave would be before the baby came. How will you soak up your *aha* moments and celebrate your harvest season?

I wondered, *Will baby girl make her appearance today?* Either way, I was enjoying this special time to myself before my life transformed forever. I was soaking up my own harvest season before my next season of planting new seeds began. For once in my life, I was trying to be present in the moment—not looking to the future—which is very hard for me to do.

But I waited too long for this chapter of my life to rush by, so I was learning to enjoy the present moment. I found myself living the life I'd prayed about, hoped for, and visualized in my darkest moments. They had been my glimmers of hope when I was barely holding on. I knew the future could look and feel different, but it took years of moving forward with faith and trust while surrendering to the path in front of me well before I could see where it would lead.

Where in your life do you need to slow down and soak up the present moment? Are you living a life you once prayed for? Even if you're not quite to your harvest season, how can you find gratitude for your courage to plant seeds and go for your big dreams? How can you find gratitude for your growing pains and your seasons of weathering storms that brought you experience, wisdom, and perspective you'd otherwise be lacking? How can you find gratitude for your harvest *before* it even comes to you? Because I promise— when you trust, let go, and surrender, it's on its way. It will most likely show up how and when you least expect it. And it will make for an incredible story.

Speaking of surrendering and allowing yourself to be surprised . . . The birth of my baby *boy* made for an incredible story to bring this book full circle.

Small Business Sister Story: Erica Boland

The Birth of a Dream: Surrendering to Faith, Fate, and New Beginnings

I saw a local woman named Shannon share that she needed volunteers to practice her reiki skills. Sign. Me. Up. I love energy and intuition and God talk and especially when they all collide. I loved everything about that first session, so I scheduled another.

In one of our early sessions, she stood over me at the head of the table and said, "I think chiropractic is a steppingstone."

It is always in hindsight we see the lessons and find clarity. I held those words from her in my heart for years because I knew deep down there was more for me too. I had been a practicing chiropractor for seven years and a doula for ten when I left a company I helped grow from a blog to a worldwide movement and enrolled in midwifery school. From the start I *knew* I would have a birth center.

After a beautiful, grueling two-plus years, I graduated from the midwifery program having been trained by a few of the best midwives in the land. One of them had been my own doula and midwife and another had also attended the birth of our youngest while the other had a surprise home birth on my grandparents-in-law's farm. So many full-circle moments and how unbelievably blessed I was. They were gracious enough to take me under their wing, and Heather and Alison of Trillium Midwifery had me as their first student.

Even while I was in midwifery school, we began looking for new business locations. We'd outgrown our current chiropractic location; I envisioned everything in one space and was falling short on finding it.

The theme *surrender* kept on coming.

We looked at so many different options, made several verbal agreements that fell through, and then I found it. The perfect location that I would make into a beautiful little birth center and women's health clinic right in the middle of our small town.

I could picture it, and I could see how the writing had been in the stars all along, and the stars were aligning perfectly.

We talked to the bank, got approved for the offer we wanted to make, and it was the day to submit the offer. Then my husband, Kyle, called. "Hey, I want you to look at a different place."

He explained he'd gotten word there may be a couple of buildings on the edge of town coming available and there'd be plenty of space for everything. But I was so frustrated. There were so many questions, we didn't even know if it would be possible to have a birth center at this location and I knew there were other offers coming in on the "perfect location."

I begrudgingly met him at this location—which, little did we know, happened to be owned by the father of our office manager. We looked around, and I just couldn't feel it. But I could tell he could.

I left and prayed to my magic person, Elise, who passed away in September of 2020. Out loud I said, "Girlfriend, send me a direct sign because I don't see it. Please make it clear."

It was the anniversary of her passing, and I shared my favorite photo of her on my Instagram. Her over the water in the state of Washington, holding a hand-painted coffee mug.

I opened Facebook Messenger later that night to a message from our office manager that said, "I'm drinking out of that same mug."

"Whaaat?!?! Where did you get that?" I was shocked.

"It's my dad's," she said.

After picking my jaw up off the floor, I laughed and thought, *Okay, sister, I hear you.* Elise had sent me just the sign I needed, and it was loud and clear.

How in the world would we turn two pole sheds into a birth center, clinic, and gym? But as I continued to surrender, one thing after another kept working out. Oh, heck yes, it was hard work and we questioned ourselves regularly, but we also trusted so deeply.

We saw our first chiropractic patients there July 1, 2024.

Stephanie and Ben were to be the first, potentially, to have their baby in the birth center, and she was due October 29.

On October 30, I woke up to one of the worst texts of my life. My preceptor I trained under, Heather Kramer, and two of her sons were killed in a head-on collision. I couldn't breathe. I couldn't wrap my head around this type of loss again. And I could not imagine showing up to a birth with such grief. The last time I saw Heather was when she stopped to see our new space to hug and congratulate me. She told me, "You did it, keep going!"

I prayed Steph and Ben's baby would wait to come until after the services.

I made it one breath and one step at a time through that next week, and Baby Ross waited too.

We waited, and waited, and waited.

As labor finally started and progressed for Steph, I did a home visit and tucked her into bed as she neared forty-two weeks. I suggested she get some semblance of rest and knew she likely wouldn't.

In the early morning hours on 11/11 (Elise's magic number), Steph absolutely rocked surrendering to the intensity of transition into motherhood. So much so that as I was looking with a mirror to see if the baby was close, the flashlight showed the baby had actually just been born!

After they were settled, I stepped out and cried.

Thank God. And . . . *holy crap!*

There was just a baby born in our birth center!

We did it! I did it! I can continue to do it.

I can hold immense joy and insurmountable grief.

I can surrender to God's plan and divine timing.

I can show up and do the work.

I can continue to listen to the pings of intuition, learn from and lean on those around me for support and walk with these families.

I can weather the seasons, learn the lessons, navigate the transitions, pivot, and stay rooted.

And I can absolutely *surrender* and see the magic.

Surrender to Be Surprised

Just like in business, I approached my birth with the desire to take the path less traveled. I knew I didn't want the traditional hospital birth experience, but I wasn't quite sure about a home birth for my first. When I heard there was a birth center opening near me right about the time I was due, I just knew that was the perfect option for me.

Along with this decision, I knew this birth would be fully unmedicated with no medical interventions offered. But with my fighter mentality, I accepted that challenge. Like all areas of my life, I wanted to *experience* birth—not numb it or intervene if at all possible. I wanted to tune into my body and intuition and let it all unfold naturally as a spiritual experience.

On Saturday, November 9, I woke up at two a.m. to the first feeling of contractions. They were mild and about ten minutes apart. I tried to go back to sleep. But at this point, I was nearing two weeks overdue. Opting for an unmedicated, intervention-free birth meant I would not be induced, so I was very excited to get things moving!

By the time Ben woke up at about seven a.m., things started escalating a bit. So we went for our usual walk with Yuka. I messaged my doula, who advised me to do the Miles Circuit again—which, if you're not familiar, is a series of movements that can help turn a baby. It's also mentally and physically exhausting, especially during contractions. But the goal is to help the baby rotate into a prime position for birth.

I was in early labor all day and night, during which we did three walks. And I was quite miserable. I was hoping that things would start to escalate Saturday night and maybe we'd meet our baby—but no such luck. Contractions were still seven to ten minutes apart.

I awoke Sunday morning—*still pregnant.* At this point, every day felt like Groundhog Day, and I was mentally and physically drained. We did another walk—this time just around the block, as I could barely make it five minutes without a contraction. As Sunday wore on, contractions finally began to intensify.

By Sunday night, we called our doula, Meghan. She came to our house and gave options for positions to help manage the pain. She told me to draw a bath and try to get some sleep because I most likely had a long night ahead of me and needed to restore my energy. At this point, I was at around forty hours of labor.

My midwife, Erica, came to check the baby's position and heart rate during my bath to see where things were at. She helped me do another inversion from my bed. I was so physically exhausted that I told her I couldn't imagine doing all this hard work without having done my workouts throughout my pregnancy, thanks to my other doula and prenatal strength training coach, Ellyn. Erica got me set up to sleep on my side. Then she told me to try and sleep through contractions. But when I got to the point where I couldn't any longer, I was to have Ben call her.

That didn't last too long. The contractions continued to intensify in strength and increased to every two to three minutes. I was officially in active labor and could hardly talk through them. Ben called Erica, and she told us it was time to head to the birth center. I felt some relief knowing we were leaving the labor stage at home and getting closer to meeting our baby!

I dreaded the car ride there and held onto Ben's hand so I could squeeze through each contraction on the way. It was still surreal at this point that we would be coming home with a baby. By the time we got to the birth center, it was almost midnight. I had prepared for a water birth, and I was so ready for the tub. I got in almost immediately, which brought some relief to my contractions.

Erica, her amazing assistant, and my doula were extremely helpful in suggesting positions that could offer the most comfort. The space itself was so relaxing—dim lights, my birth playlist playing, and everything I'd hoped for to relax my mind and body into the present moment.

Before too long, I started feeling the urge to push. Erica checked me to see how far I was, and I'm grateful I never actually knew. I was just intuitively listening to my body. Through every part of this experience, my birth team kept telling me to listen to my body— which is exactly what I wanted for my birth.

When I told them I felt ready to push, Erica told me to just let everything go in doing so—to not hold anything back. I did just that in the next contraction, and it felt like a total surrender. My breathing continued to carry me through each wave of intensity, which made me so grateful for all my prep work in hypnobirthing, meditation, and breath work.

I started to feel like I couldn't labor any longer in the tub. I was losing my energy, and it was getting harder to summon the strength I needed to hold my head out of the water. I was physically exhausted, but I knew if I got out, it would be more painful. I intuitively knew I was so close to meeting our baby, so I told myself to power through mentally, surrender it all, and let go. Again, so much of what I had learned in my years of pursuing entrepreneurship, training for MMA, and building mental resilience continued to pay off in this moment.

So I squeezed Ben's hands for one more total surrender through the next contraction, and I felt complete *relief*—baby was out! They told me to reach down to feel the baby's head, but I replied, "No, I think she's out!" Baby came out so fast that they weren't expecting it. We immediately pulled the baby out of the water and onto my chest to soak up the sweetest moments.

We rested, I fed the baby, and we all conversed about how crazy fast that was. Ben got to cut the cord, and as they were going to grab the baby off my chest, I looked up to the biggest surprise of my life and exclaimed, "*That's a boy!*"

We were in shock and disbelief, especially because my intuition had been right—once again. I *knew* I was destined to be a boy mom.

Ben hugged him and said, "My little champ!"

So there he was, the biggest, best surprise we could have never imagined. Coming in at eight pounds even and twenty inches, he was as healthy as could be. So, now what were we going to name him?

We had chosen the name Valerie Rose after our gender reveal party, and my heart was set on that! I mean, I had been journaling to Val for almost five months. So, after some discussion, we chose to keep the name Valory.

We combined the words *valor* and the name Valerie. His name means health, vitality, strength, and courage. Valory was born at 2:13 a.m., and we left the birth center by 5:30 a.m. with a baby *boy* in our hands on 11/11, which is a very special day. The number 11-11 has a strong spiritual meaning behind it. Some believe it's a sign that angels or spiritual guides are nearby, offering support and encouragement, and others believe it's associated with the start of a new phase or journey in life. It's known to be a reminder to pause, reflect, and be present in the moment.

I have immense gratitude for my amazing birth team, which encouraged, supported, and allowed me to have a spiritual, intervention-free birth experience. Valory was the first baby to be born at Coulee Health Birth Collective, and I had the birth I'd hoped and prayed for. And it all ended with the biggest and best surprise of my life—an incredibly handsome little boy.

I walked away from the entire transformation into motherhood, realizing how incredible the female body is. It is inspiring to witness what we are capable of when we put in the preparation but also learn to trust, surrender, and let go throughout the process—just as I have in my businesses.

I, of course, had doubts and fears about whether I could handle this level of pain and total surrender. But I continued to focus on controlling what I could—my mind, body, and soul. While this birth experience might not be for every woman, I think we far too often discount our ability to do the thing our bodies were designed to innately do without needing modern medical intervention. We are so much *stronger* than we give ourselves credit for.

While I would have loved to skip the forty hours of early labor, I still wouldn't change a thing, as it was all part of our journey to meet the baby boy who made it all worth it.

Why do I share my birth story? Because through my entire pregnancy, birth experience, and postpartum period, I continued to realize how much my journey into motherhood reminded me of my journey in small business ownership. There was a literal seed planted that grew and carried me through many challenges, mentally and physically. And on the other side was this amazing baby boy who made all the hard work, effort, sacrifices, and changes worth it.

The birth of my first business was a journey.

The birth of my first baby was a journey.

They were both hard in their own ways. They both gave me wisdom, perspective, experience, and lessons that I have carried with me along the way.

Every time I've faced what felt like an insurmountable challenge or setback along my journey, I've laughed and said, "This is going to make a great chapter in my book someday!"

When we were surprised during Val's birth story—being that he was a boy—I just knew this was the final story that was going to make a great chapter in this very book you are reading today. I couldn't have asked for a better story to complete this season of my life, from planting, growing, weathering, and harvesting in entrepreneurship to starting all over in a new season of motherhood.

Chapter Reflections

Reflection Questions:

- ❖ Where are you gripping too tightly to an outcome?
- ❖ How has an experience or relationship come full circle in your business or life?
- ❖ How can you surrender and allow yourself to be surprised by how your harvest season shows up for you?

Intentional Action:

- New Small Business Owner: Obviously, you have not experienced your harvest season yet in your small business. You just started! So, my advice is to simply grow in your patience for your harvest season. Embrace your growth circle of small business ownership and take all the lessons from this book with you to support and guide you along your journey. Find your community to support you along the way. Being a soul-preneur will be the most transformative experience you'll ever embark on.

- Seasoned Small Business Owner: If you are in a harvest season, soak it up and find gratitude every day for the journey that got you there. Eventually, it will be time to dream some new dreams. But savor the present moment and all the hard work it took to get you there. If you're not in your harvest season yet, stay open to what's on its way to you. Regardless, I encourage you to take what I call a "getaway day" to get out of your business and go somewhere that inspires you. I love to find a cute little town no more than an hour's drive away where I can find a coffee shop, somewhere to walk outside, and maybe even a few cute shops so I can treat myself. Whatever you decide to do, allow yourself the freedom to follow your own curiosity, get back to dreaming about your vision, and see what signs show up for you. I have had entire afternoons of simply doing whatever sounded fun. The places they have led me to and the people I have met because I chose to just surrender and stay open are purely divine intervention. Last, but certainly not least, help and support other small business owners in their planting, growing, or weathering-the-storm season when you can, just as you would have loved to help in your own growth seasons.

So what's your story? What stories and experiences will be the best chapters in the story of your life and business someday? What season of your circle of growth are you currently in? How can it help someone else in their journey?

My journey isn't anything special. I just decided to share it. I firmly believe we all have stories to share from different seasons of our lives and that it's part of our soul's purpose to put it out into the world.

What do I want you to do with this book? Take time to reflect on your own story, then show up and share it! Whether it's with one person or the whole world—you decide. But what is the point of life if we don't find the purpose in it? I've always said that if sharing my own struggles and successes could help *one* person, having gone through it would serve its purpose. Do the same. Share your story to help just one person feel less alone in their own season of soul-preneurship.

How you choose to share is up to you, but don't let the stories of your seasons of planting, growing, weathering storms, and harvesting go untold. You just never know who might be inspired to show up for their own journey and feel less alone in the season they're in.

As I close the chapter on this past decade and step into a new cycle and season of my life and business, I am reflecting on all the ways the journey has shaken me, shaped me, and surprised me. But none of it broke me. I can see now in the rearview mirror how it was all meant to be.

Every season prepares you for the next one, so you must learn to embrace the one you are in while looking forward to the future. And that's because your best self isn't found in the future. It's in your day-to-day decisions. It's when you're deciding to show up when it's hard. Deciding to stay consistent when you don't feel like you are making progress. Deciding to make hard decisions when you know they're the right ones for you. Deciding to listen and lean into your intuition.

Every day, we make an average of 35,000 decisions. I sure am glad you chose to pick up this book and read this far.

As for me, I am embracing this new season of mom-preneurship while I look forward to planting new seeds for the future.

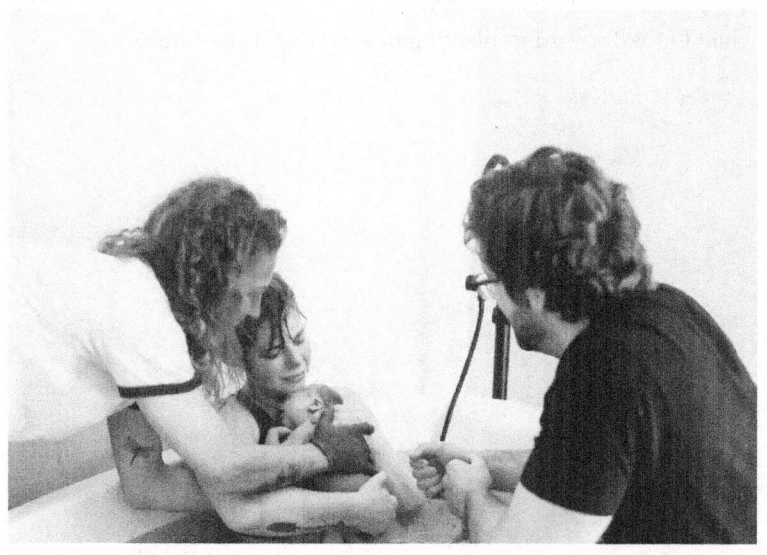

Valory's Birth with midwife Dr. Erica & Ben on 11-11 (2024)

Call to Action

Wow, what a journey it has been. I'm so immensely grateful that you followed this circle of growth with me from seed to harvest on my small business journey. I would *love* to stay connected so I can support you on your own soul-preneur journey!

There are many ways to stay connected with me and my Small Business Sister Circle™ community.

Scan the code below to:

- Sign up for my email list to receive updates on the book, additional resources, and opportunities to connect with me
- Find a book club guide so you can read this book along with a community
- Listen to *new* podcast episodes
- Learn more about joining me and my fellow small business sisters inside Sister Circle Membership for a supportive community and top-notch small business education each month
- Submit your own story and share how this book has positively impacted you
- Book me to speak at your upcoming event in person or virtually
- And so much more

I can't wait to connect with you. I'm cheering for you, sis!

Love, Steph

stephanie
lea ♥ ross

Scan the code for all
Book Bonus Resources!

Author Bio

Stephanie Ross is a seasoned business educator, enthusiastic community leader, and empowering speaker dedicated to helping female entrepreneurs build thriving, soul-driven businesses. With more than a decade of hands-on experience, she founded her fitness and yoga studio at just 20 years old, scaling it into a successful six-figure business. Throughout her entrepreneurial journey, Stephanie encountered significant obstacles, yet these challenges inspired her to pivot and create Small Business Sister Circle™—a vibrant community where women can connect, learn, and grow profitable, sustainable businesses together.

Through her podcast, she shares authentic conversations and practical wisdom, empowering women to align their business with their deeper purpose. Whether coaching, speaking, or leading community experiences, Stephanie brings warmth, passion, and resilience to every interaction, leaving others motivated and inspired to design a business and life they truly love.

Learn more about Stephanie and her mission at: stephanieleaross.com.